100 PLANES 100 YEARS

THE FIRST CENTURY OF AVIATION

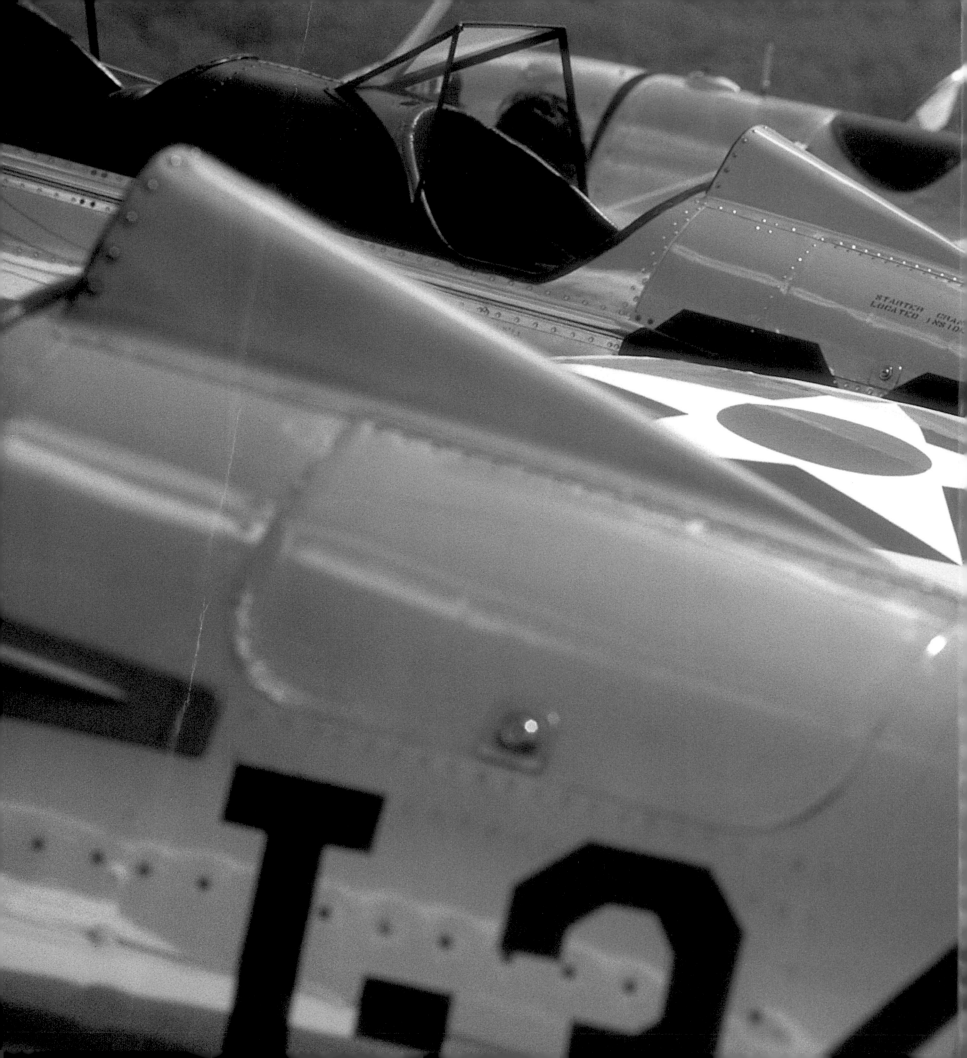

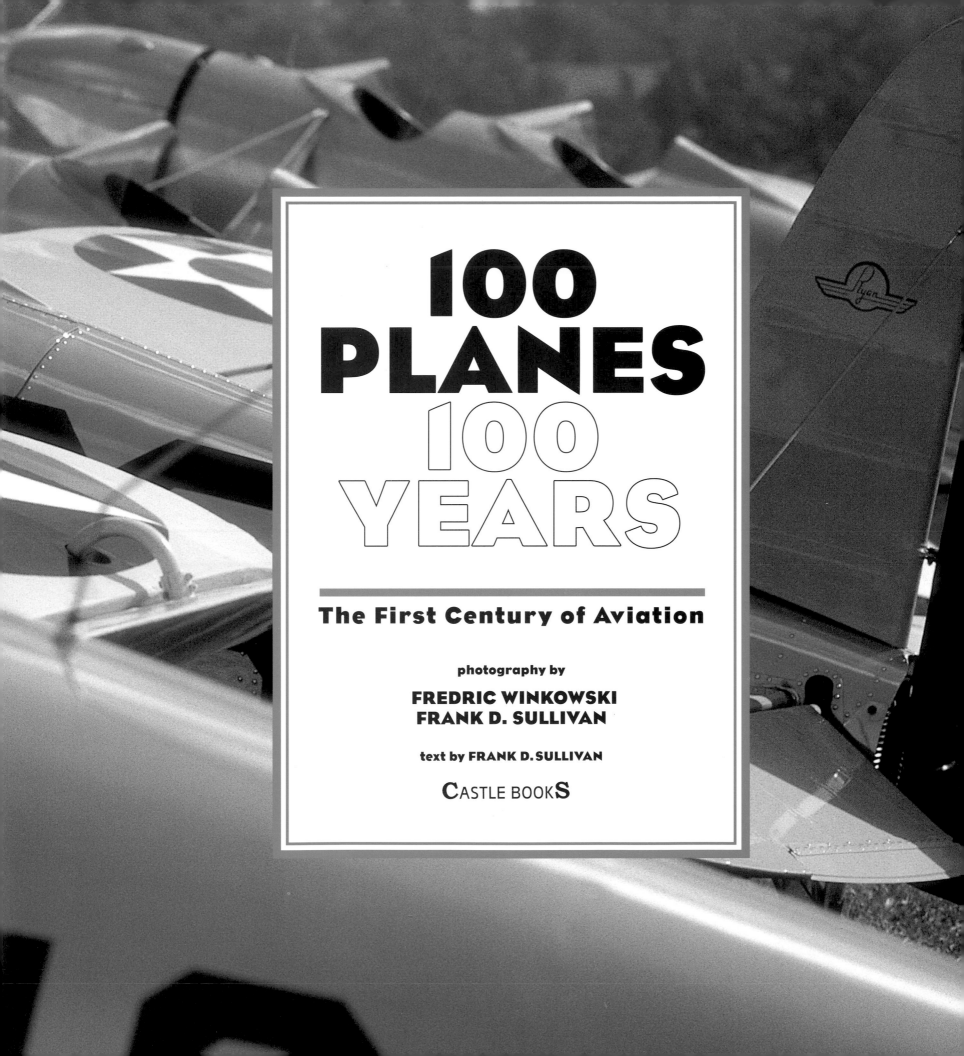

100 PLANES
100 YEARS

The First Century of Aviation

photography by

FREDRIC WINKOWSKI
FRANK D. SULLIVAN

text by **FRANK D. SULLIVAN**

CASTLE BOOKS

This edition published in 2003 by

CASTLE BOOKS ®
A division of Book Sales, Inc.
114 Northfield Avenue
Edison, New Jersey 08837

Published by arrangement with
Frederic Winkowski Photo Publications
48 West 71st Street
New York, New York 10023

10 9 8 7 6 5 4 3 2 1

Library of Congress Cataloging-in-Publication Data

Winkowski, Fred.
    100 planes, 100 years : the first century of aviation / Frederic
  Winkowski and Frank D. Sullivan.
        p.   cm.
    Includes index.
    1. Airplanes—History. 2. Aeronautics—History. 3. Airplanes—
Collectors and collecting. I. Sullivan, Frank, 1942-   . II. Title.
  TL670.3.W55   1988   98-7450
  629.13'09—dc21   CIP

ISBN: 0-7858-1671-2   Printed in China

C O N T E N T S

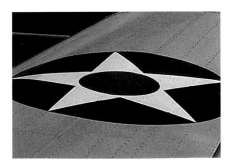

INTRODUCTION

The Airplane...Its First Hundred Years

The story of aviation and the history of the twentieth century are inseparable. From the Wright brothers' little known early manned gliders of 1900, through the armadas of warplanes in two world wars, to today's airborne "people movers", the progress of aircraft development has helped define the various epochs of the last one hundred years.

Now at century's end, it is appropriate to look back in time, to examine each year from 1900 until 2000, and remember the airplanes that helped write the history of our times across the skies.

The Chronology

The authors have considered each year since 1900 and selected one classic airplane or family of planes which made history that year. Our selection criteria were based on historical importance, uniqueness, and simple availability of surviving models, but without a doubt, "excitement" was our bottom line. Excitement, in terms of visual appeal and an exciting story to be told. We selected types that we ourselves have photographed, most of which are still flying or are preserved in museum collections. Although the airplane chosen for a particular year may not be the obvious one, our occasionally offbeat choices always highlight some milestone in aviation history. In some cases, the plane portrayed may be representative of a type or family of planes that may not exist any longer.

For those who take notice of such things, there are more than one hundred aircraft illustrated in this book. Sometimes there are so many types to choose from that we show families of craft such as deHavilland or Sopwith planes, or planes that are usually mentioned in the same breath, such as the Hurricane and Spitfire, or the F-86 Saber and MiG-15. Some choices were just too difficult. Covering the W.W.II years especially seemed too restrictive. Could six airplanes really represent all that happened in those world spanning battles? Additionally, so many beautiful examples of these planes are still flying. So please don't hold us too tightly to our book's title, instead enjoy with us the abundance of preserved aircraft ....

This is not anyone's top 100 list; our choices are meant to surprise or at least give pause . Some of these craft had one brief year of glory. A surprising number served for more than half the century. Some will continue on unforseeably far into the 21st Century. This trend to longevity will likely continue in both military and civil aircraft.

The Survivors
It is a pure accident of technology that the oldest aircraft extant are, most times, the easiest to keep flying. So it is that Bleriots and Curtiss Pushers can be kept in the air on a shoestring by cash-strapped organizations such as the Rhinebeck Aerodrome, while even the richly endowed (by

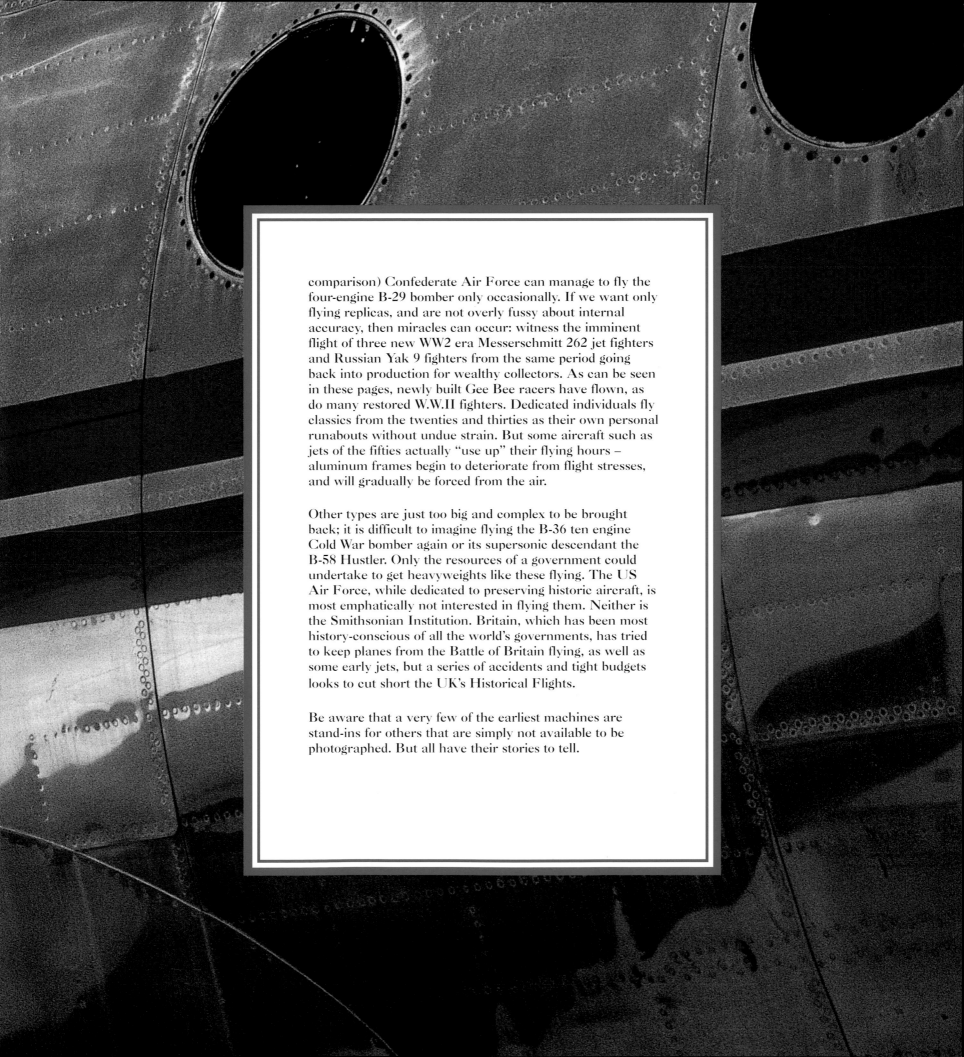

comparison) Confederate Air Force can manage to fly the
four-engine B-29 bomber only occasionally. If we want only
flying replicas, and are not overly fussy about internal
accuracy, then miracles can occur: witness the imminent
flight of three new WW2 era Messerschmitt 262 jet fighters
and Russian Yak 9 fighters from the same period going
back into production for wealthy collectors. As can be seen
in these pages, newly built Gee Bee racers have flown, as
do many restored W.W.II fighters. Dedicated individuals fly
classics from the twenties and thirties as their own personal
runabouts without undue strain. But some aircraft such as
jets of the fifties actually "use up" their flying hours –
aluminum frames begin to deteriorate from flight stresses,
and will gradually be forced from the air.

Other types are just too big and complex to be brought
back; it is difficult to imagine flying the B-36 ten engine
Cold War bomber again or its supersonic descendant the
B-58 Hustler. Only the resources of a government could
undertake to get heavyweights like these flying. The US
Air Force, while dedicated to preserving historic aircraft, is
most emphatically not interested in flying them. Neither is
the Smithsonian Institution. Britain, which has been most
history-conscious of all the world's governments, has tried
to keep planes from the Battle of Britain flying, as well as
some early jets, but a series of accidents and tight budgets
looks to cut short the UK's Historical Flights.

Be aware that a very few of the earliest machines are
stand-ins for others that are simply not available to be
photographed. But all have their stories to tell.

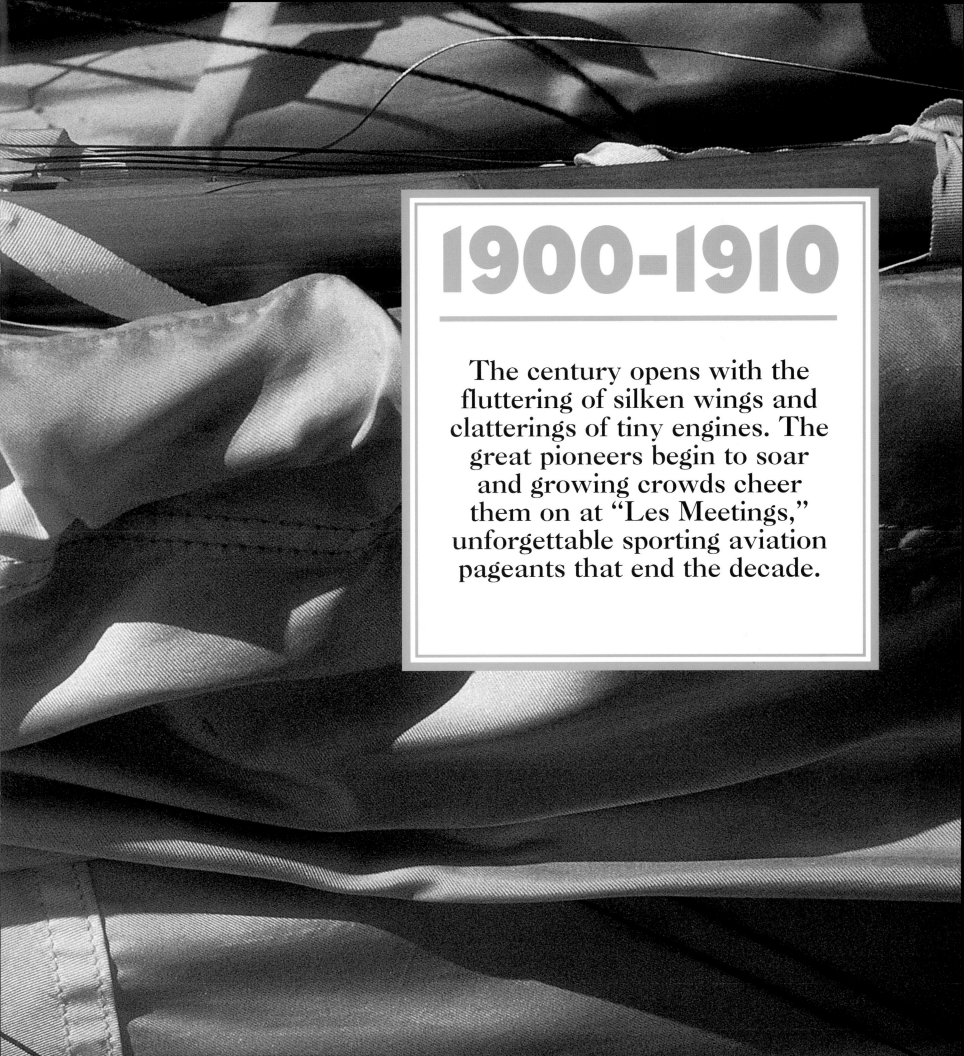

1900-1910

The century opens with the fluttering of silken wings and clatterings of tiny engines. The great pioneers begin to soar and growing crowds cheer them on at "Les Meetings," unforgettable sporting aviation pageants that end the decade.

1901
Whitehead Airplane No. 21

Controversy surrounds this strange looking flying machine. Some say that Gustave Whitehead flew on August 14, 1901, thus beating the Wright Brothers' claim; others say even if he got into the air, his craft would have been uncontrollable and the distances claimed by witnesses were misstatements or worse. The original craft no longer exists, but preserved in Fairfield, Connecticut, is this beautiful replica of the Whitehead flyer which was taken out of storage by its owner and builder Andrew Kosch especially for our photos.

Short flights were made in 1986 in Bridgeport, Connecticut with Kosch as pilot, using modern ultralight engines and landing gear, but with most other materials, notably bamboo and Japanese silk, as per the original. The fuselage is very heavily constructed just as Whitehead's was, with solid wood wheels that have their own engine. Dummy engines and props are mounted on the replica. Whitehead's original engines were remarkable. He built two-cylinder acetylene "steam type" power units for this plane, and later manufactured aircraft engines commercally for other experimenters .

Enthusiasts in Germany, Whitehead's birthplace, are attempting to fly a near-duplicate of the Whitehead plane as this is written. Though the Wrights' achievments stand on their own, Whitehead's graceful, birdlike creation seems a fitting symbol for the tentative beginnings of powered flight.

1902
Chanute Glider

In October, 1902, when the Wright Brothers concluded their successful glider trials at Kill Devil Hills, on hand as witness was Octave Chanute. The 70-year-old Chanute had pioneered the art of hang gliding, though he didn't fly himself. Since 1896, he and associate Augustus Herring had been experimenting with a series of biplane gliders like the one pictured here. Though this is a 1905 model, Chanute's most successful gliders were much alike. The biplane wings, one above the other, could be braced and trussed, bridge-like, with struts and cross wires—not surprising since Chanute had been an architect and bridge builder earlier in his life. In these gliders, the pilot hangs from the lower wings, using his feet as landing gear and twisting his body for control, exactly like today's colorful hang gliders.

Originally, Chanute had merely been content to document the history and compile the scientific literature of aeronautics, but he later succumbed to the lure of building his own apparatus, using German gliding pioneer Otto Lilienthal's work as point of departure. He went on to become the grand old man of flight, nurturing many other budding tinkerers all over the U.S. The Wrights began writing to him in 1900, beginning a warm friendship and exchanging ideas freely. However, they distrusted the hang glider concept, choosing instead a prone pilot position and movable controls for their superior machines.

1903-1904

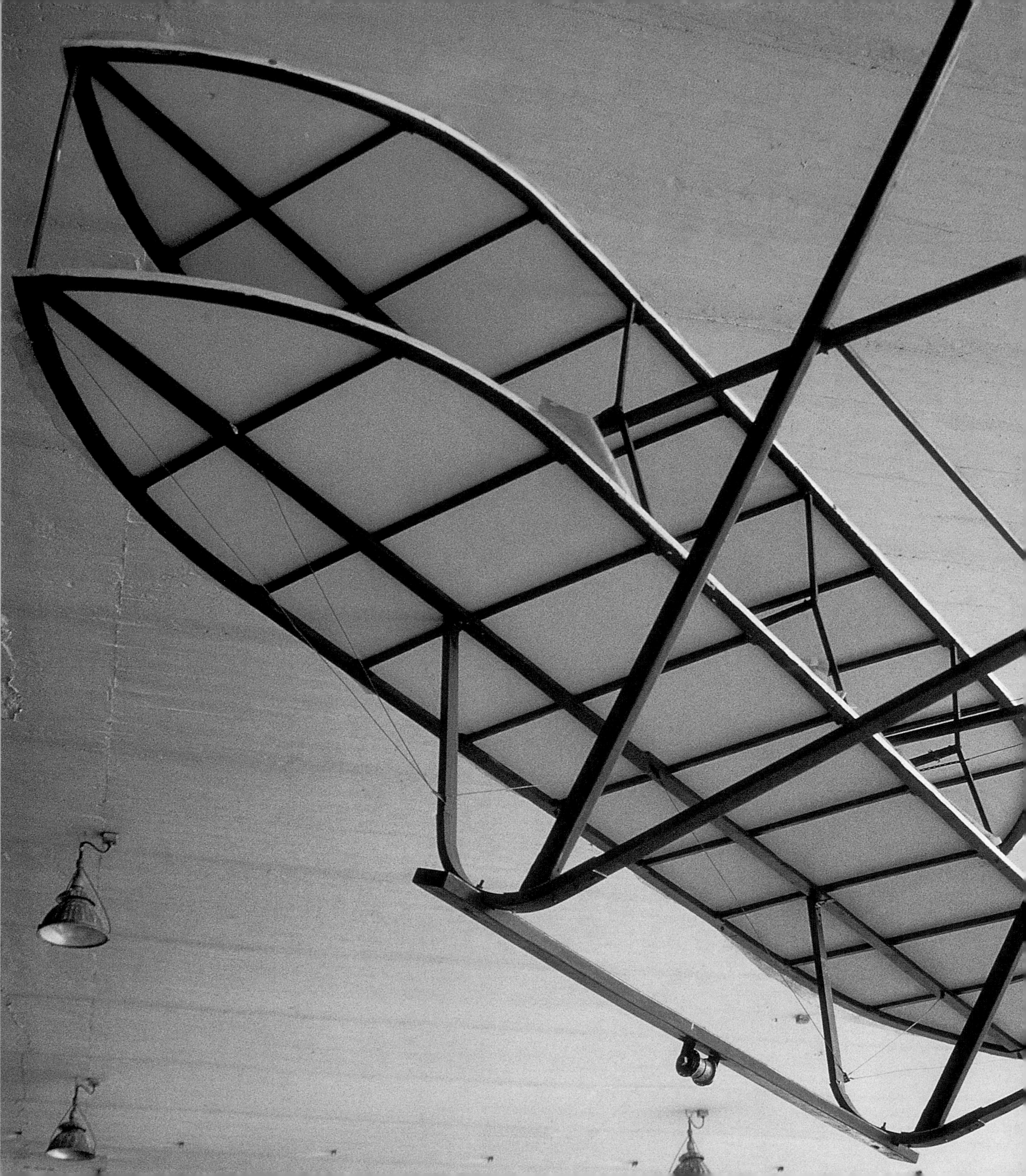

1903
Wright Flyer

"Success four flights Thursday morning..." The telegram sent to the Wrights' father tersely notes that Orville and Wilbur realized the significance of their accomplishment that icy December day on the dunes of Kitty Hawk. But to them that landmark day was merely a data point in an unbroken series of experiments and research begun before the century's turn. In fact, the little Wright Flyer, wrecked after that day's last flight, was cannibalized for future models, each a stepwise improvement over the last, until by October 1905, half-hour flights were the norm. That first day of powered flights, none lasting more than a minute, was the result of a sequence of quick but brilliant and groundbreaking excursions into the sciences of airfoil design, wind tunnel testing, propeller theory, and combustion engine manufacture.

Perhaps most important, the brothers taught themselves to fly. Unlike in Europe where flight was thought to be a simple matter of "mounting and riding" an air vehicle much as one would an automobile, the Wrights realized that flying was a skill to be honed by hours of practice. They learned from "The Flying Man," Otto Lilienthal, and mentor Octave Chanute, but used their own separate movable control surfaces for each axis of motion. This proved to be the key to practical controlled powered flight.

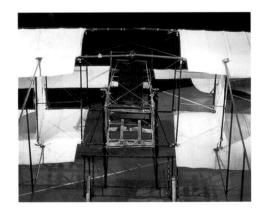

1904
Voisin Biplane

In 1904, France was possibly the country most obsessed with flight; hearing rumors of the Wrights' successes, French aeronauts were galvanized into action. In April of this year, a wealthy and well-connected Parisian lawyer and sportsman, Ernest Archdeacon, and aerial experimenter Captain Ferdinand Ferber hired two brothers to help solve the problems of powered flight. Gabriel and Charles Voisin had been experimenting with gliders since 1898. Working mainly with Ferber, they adapted the basic Wright layout, with a boxkite wing design similar to that developed by the Australian kite-builder, Hargrave. The brothers Voisin understood little of the Wrights' control methods, but after much tinkering and many dead ends, they managed their first powered flight in 1907. Well satisfied with their results, the Voisins had the cheek to set up a production line for these marginal machines. More than twenty were sold by 1909 to some of France's most famous aviators: Henry Farman, Leon Delagrange, even U.S. escape artist Harry Houdini had one. Most were personalized with the owner's name in large letters on the tail.

The Voisin in the photographs is an extremely rare machine from the Rhinebeck collection.

1905
Curtiss Pusher

On the Fourth of July 1905, the first dirigible ever seen over New York flew around Coney Island and Brighton Beach. Captain Thomas Baldwin's "California Arrow" airship was powered by a Glenn Curtiss engine. These engines, made light and reliable for the down-in-the-dirt sport of motorcycle racing, were perfect for aircraft, as Baldwin had quickly realized .

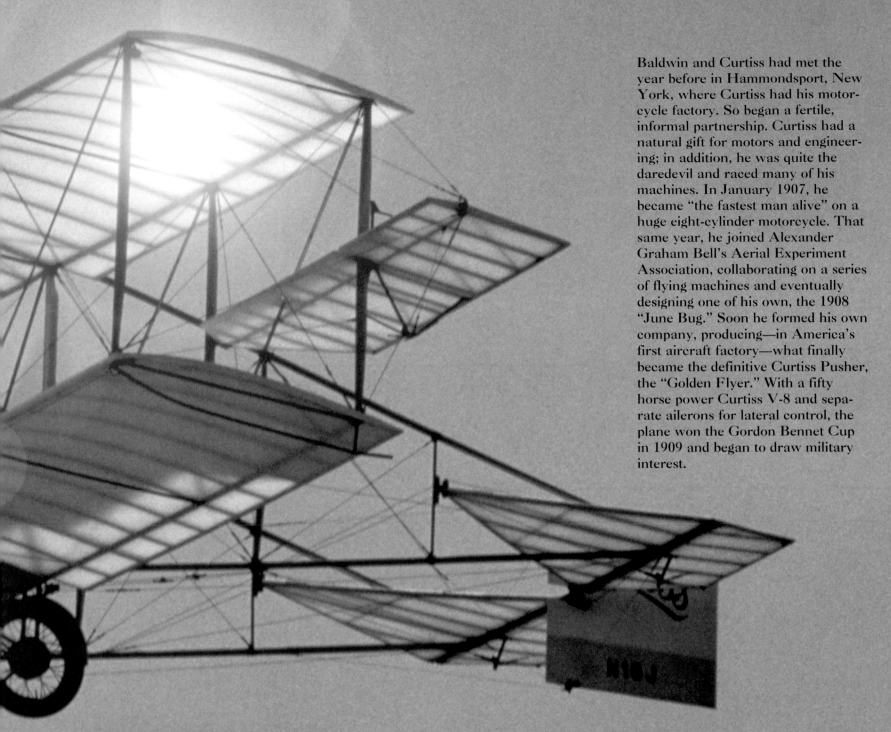

Baldwin and Curtiss had met the year before in Hammondsport, New York, where Curtiss had his motorcycle factory. So began a fertile, informal partnership. Curtiss had a natural gift for motors and engineering; in addition, he was quite the daredevil and raced many of his machines. In January 1907, he became "the fastest man alive" on a huge eight-cylinder motorcycle. That same year, he joined Alexander Graham Bell's Aerial Experiment Association, collaborating on a series of flying machines and eventually designing one of his own, the 1908 "June Bug." Soon he formed his own company, producing—in America's first aircraft factory—what finally became the definitive Curtiss Pusher, the "Golden Flyer." With a fifty horse power Curtiss V-8 and separate ailerons for lateral control, the plane won the Gordon Bennet Cup in 1909 and began to draw military interest.

By 1910, stunt pilots such as the great Lincoln Beachey cavorting over farmers' fields and small towns in machines like the Curtiss Pusher shown here were inventing the sport of barnstorming, and the Curtiss Company was giving the less-innovative Wrights a run for their money.

17

1906
Santos Dumont Demoiselle

Albert Santos Dumont had been an aeronaut since before the turn of the century, building and flying lighter-than-air craft. In 1901, he maneuvered one of these airships around the Eiffel Tower and instantly became the toast of Paris. The Brazilian-born inventor then turned his hand to heavier-than-air machines in 1906. Inspired partly by stories of the Wright Brothers' planes, he built an odd boxkite-type machine dubbed by him "the 14 bis," but the crowds called it the "canard," or duck, because of its long-necked, tail-first appearance. With this just-barely-flyable craft and good press coverage, Santos claimed both the Archdeacon Prize for the first 25 meter flight and the Aero Club de France prize of 1,500 Francs for a 100 meter flight.

What is shown here, however, is a replica of the aircraft for which Santos became best known. In 1907, he began to develop and fly what was really the world's first ultra-light plane. With a tiny wingspan of less than 17 feet and a 35 hp motor, the petite Demoiselle, or "dragonfly," was, and really still is, the minimum necessary to get a pilot aloft. The Demoiselle became the choice of sportsmen, with ten or fifteen being built, but Santos never flew again after 1909, becoming progressively ill with multiple sclerosis. He died in 1932.

1907
Antoinette VII Monoplane

Although no Antoinette aircraft was to fly until 1908, by 1907 the appealingly named company produced innovative motorboat engines that were the choice of many French

airmen. In August and September 1907, two seminal helicopter designs, both using Antoinette engines, made short hops. In November, Louis Bleriot, soon to gain fame as the first to fly the English Channel, flew his first tractor monoplane, which, like most of his earlier designs, used an Antoinette 50 HP V-8.

When Antoinette designer Leon Levasseur finally got his own machine to fly, it was a beautiful craft, and for good reason, since engineer Levasseur had trained as an artist. When one of his creations appeared at "Le Meeting" near Rheims, France, in 1909, an English woman named Gertrude Bacon saw it in flight and entered this rhapsodic description in her diary: " A dragon-fly, a darting graceful immensely powerful dragonfly...the beautiful white wings and flashing propellors stood out as a dream of pure loveliness."

Look closely: the Antoinette VII pictured here is actually a model built to the scale of 1/6 of an inch to one foot. The three surviving authentic Antoinettes that we know of all are hanging from museum ceilings.

1908
Hanriot
Monoplane

In 1908, while the Antoinette mono-planes were making their first flights, a racing car driver named Rene Hanriot was hard at work building a similar craft. The finished mono-plane was duly exhibited at the 1909 Salon in Paris, the first great avia-tion exhibit. By 1910, Hanriot was operating a flying school at Betheny,

near Rheims. When his fifteen-year-old son Marcel received his license there in June 1910, he became the world's youngest pilot.

Never quite as graceful looking as the Antoinettes, the typical Hanriot monoplane at this time had that same racing-scull-with-wings look—the fuselage was built like a boat hull, using marine mahogany plywood. Pilot, engine, and fuel tank all sat on rather than in the fuselage, as demon-strated perfectly by this flying replica from Rhinebeck, New York.

Later Hanriot monoplanes resembled early Nieuports like the one shown for the year 1912. This was no accident, since they employed the same designer, but the day of the monoplane was over as suddenly as it had dawned. They were seen as unsafe, so military contracts went to biplanes in both England and France. Rene Hanriot left the aviation busi-ness for a few years, but later with partner Pierre Dupont produced a standout biplane fighter called the HD.1, used by Belgian World War I flying ace Willy Coppens.

1908

The English Channel had been the impassable moat guarding Great Britain since 1066, but in July 1909, it was breached by this improbably small and frail monoplane. So simple and pure an expression of flight did this craft seem to ordinary people, that it became an icon of its time. The Bleriot appeared on posters, ceramics, and as little toys and knick-knacks. One hundred thousand people saw the machine on display at Selfridge's department store in London after the Channel flight. The plane can be endearing even today, as this restored 1910 Bleriot XI—the oldest flying airplane in the U.S.—shows, as it skims briefly into Rhinebeck, New York, skies. "We can fly!" says the little white cross-shaped Bleriot.

The builder-pilot of the Channel-crossing machine, Louis Bleriot, seemed himself improbably cast as daredevil pilot, though he had walked away from his share of wrecks. He was a successful businessman who had plowed all of a substantial fortune into a series of ten previous aircraft with little success, until the type XI. He refined his type VII tractor monoplane concept using wing warping controls, an efficient prop, and a reliable—though improbable-looking and low-powered—engine: the 3-cylinder, fan-shaped Anzani. Bleriot's prize-winning flight, though more significant politically and militarily than for its duration, was no fluke. The Bleriot XI went into production, and served French and British forces through the early stages of World War I.

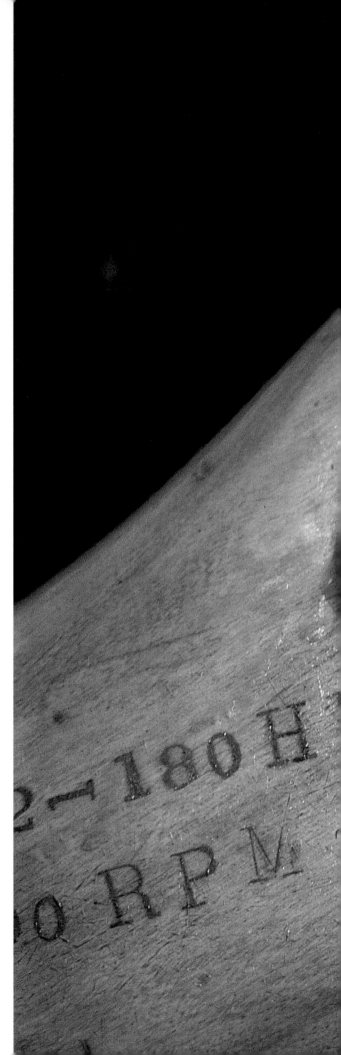

1910
Avro Triplane

An imposing entry at the London Olympia Aero Show in 1910 was the "Mercury" triplane built by Alliott Vernon Roe. Slated to appear at the Blackpool show in July, two were destroyed en route in a railway fire. Quickly, replacements were assembled and after the Blackpool appearance, they went on to a successful tour of America.

The 1911 Roe IV pictured here at the Shuttleworth hangars was really an improved Mercury with larger span upper wings. This one is a flying replica built for the 1965 movie *"Those Magnificent Men in their Flying Machines,"* where it was flown by the evil Sir Percy Ware-Armitage as played by Terry Thomas.

A. V. Roe, whose creations were almost always called "Avros," started out small in aviation, with a prize winning model airplane in 1907. He soon made the triplane his specialty but was usually strapped for cash, so was forced to use tiny 6 HP and 9HP engines. It was not until the Avro 500 series that Roe hit his stride– see the entry for 1913– and built the company that produced the WW II Lancaster bomber and the giant delta winged Vulcan jet.

1910-1919

An innocent age of racing and record setting sparks the first timid warplane designs and plane makers struggle to keep up with the fang and claw evolution of the World War. A new weapon and a new mythology of individual air combat is born.

1911 Deperdussin Schneider Racer

A deceptively idyllic scene at Thorpe Park in England as a replica of the 1913 Schneider trophy-winning Deperdussin float plane rests at a lakeside mooring. At the time of its victory, the Deperdussin monoplane represented aviation's peak of speed and power. Not until twenty years later would monoplanes regain their ascendency.

In 1911, the Deperdussin firm had built several successful monoplanes, but late that year designer Louis Bechereau applied new wood forming techniques to producing stream-lined airplane fuselages. Using the strong light molded plywood to form a perfect teardrop shape behind the enclosed double row 160 HP rotary, the whole capped by a hemispherical prop spinner, Bechereau had a winner. The new monoplane was unbeatable! The 1912 and 1913 Gordon Bennett cups went to the Deperdussin Monocoques which now routinely surpassed two miles per minute. At the first Schneider trophy race for seaplanes in Monaco in April 1913, things did not go as planned, however. The new plane built for the race blew its engine, so pilot Maurice Prevost flew an older model with floats braced by a forest of struts as shown in the photo, and still he won, even after being forced to re-fly ten kilometers of the course. The Deperdussin company foundered despite these triumphs, due to financial scandals, but designer Bechereau landed on his feet, going on to reorganize the company that would come to be known as SPAD.

1912
Nieuport IIN Monoplane

The Nieuport Monoplane's jaunty, deep-keeled fuselage design was the look dominating sport and racing aviation in the years right before World War I. In 1910, Edouard de Nieport's designer, a Monsieur Pagny, was one of the first to enclose the pilot and engine in this type of streamlined fuselage. Pagny later designed similar machines for manufacturers Hanriot and Ponnier, after a Nieuport won the Gordon Bennet Race in 1911. By 1912, Nieuports routinely flew over 100 mph, and on Valentine's Day that year, a British Army engineer, Lt. B.H. Barrington-Kennett, won £500 by flying just under 250 miles nonstop.

One of Rhinebeck Aerodrome's earliest replicas, this pretty red Nieuport IIN was photographed in New York City on the occasion of Cartier's introduction of the Santos watch in 1979.

1913
Avro 504

When the first prototype Avro 504 placed only fourth in the 1913 British Aerial Derby, builder A.V. Roe thought it was a bad omen; he might be lucky to sell six. Surprisingly, the stalky, two-place biplane was produced in the thousands, more than any other British World War I type.

Never too speedy, the long wings of the Avro could lift the plane high and far by the standards of early World War I. This enabled the first Royal Naval Air Service 504's reaching the front to undertake dangerous and celebrated long range bombing missions, notably to the Zeppelin sheds at Lake Constance and the submarine slips near Antwerp. But the 504's foremost task was as a trainer. Virtually every British flier from mid-war through the mid-twenties, including the future King George VI, learned on one. The 504 was fully aerobatic but forgiving of student error. Its rotary engine gave an inkling of what demanding airplanes like the Camel and the Snipe had in store.

This restored original 504K, most numerous of all the Avro variants, flew at Shuttleworth during the late 1970s in the khaki drab finish used by the British after 1916. The RAF's red, white, and blue roundel marking makes the first of many appearances here.

1914
Royal Aircraft
Factory FE-8

The pusher fighter concept was viable, even innovative—since armament of any kind was a novelty in military craft—when the FE-2 was ordered in 1914. By mid-1916, when the two-seat FE-2 was joined by the single seat FE-8 and the similar deHavilland DH-2, they were considered antiquated, and about to meet their nemesis, the Albatros, over the Somme.

The original FE-8, as portrayed here by a flying replica from Owl's Head, Maine, flew in 1915, but represents a whole generation of British fighting aircraft. Descending from the original Voisin and Farman pusher types, they enabled pilots to fire a fixed gun straight forward without hitting the propeller. Some pusher fighters such as the FE-8 and the DH-2 enjoyed a brief heyday and fought well against the Fokker monoplanes. When synchronizing gear was perfected, these types were instantly obsolete, since the new types could now fire through their props and no longer needed the clumsy pusher layout. Even so, FE-8s fought on for more than a year.

Only the suicidally aggressive tactics adapted by British Royal Flying Corps. fighter units gained them any advantage in the one-sided battles fought by squadrons flying the "Fee"— as the FE-8 was nicknamed. Standing Orders were: "Attack everything!" By March 1917, when German ace Baron von Richthofen's flight, flying the Albatros III, shot down five out of nine FE-8's from Forty Squadron in minutes, during the Battle of the Somme, this tactic had become total folly.

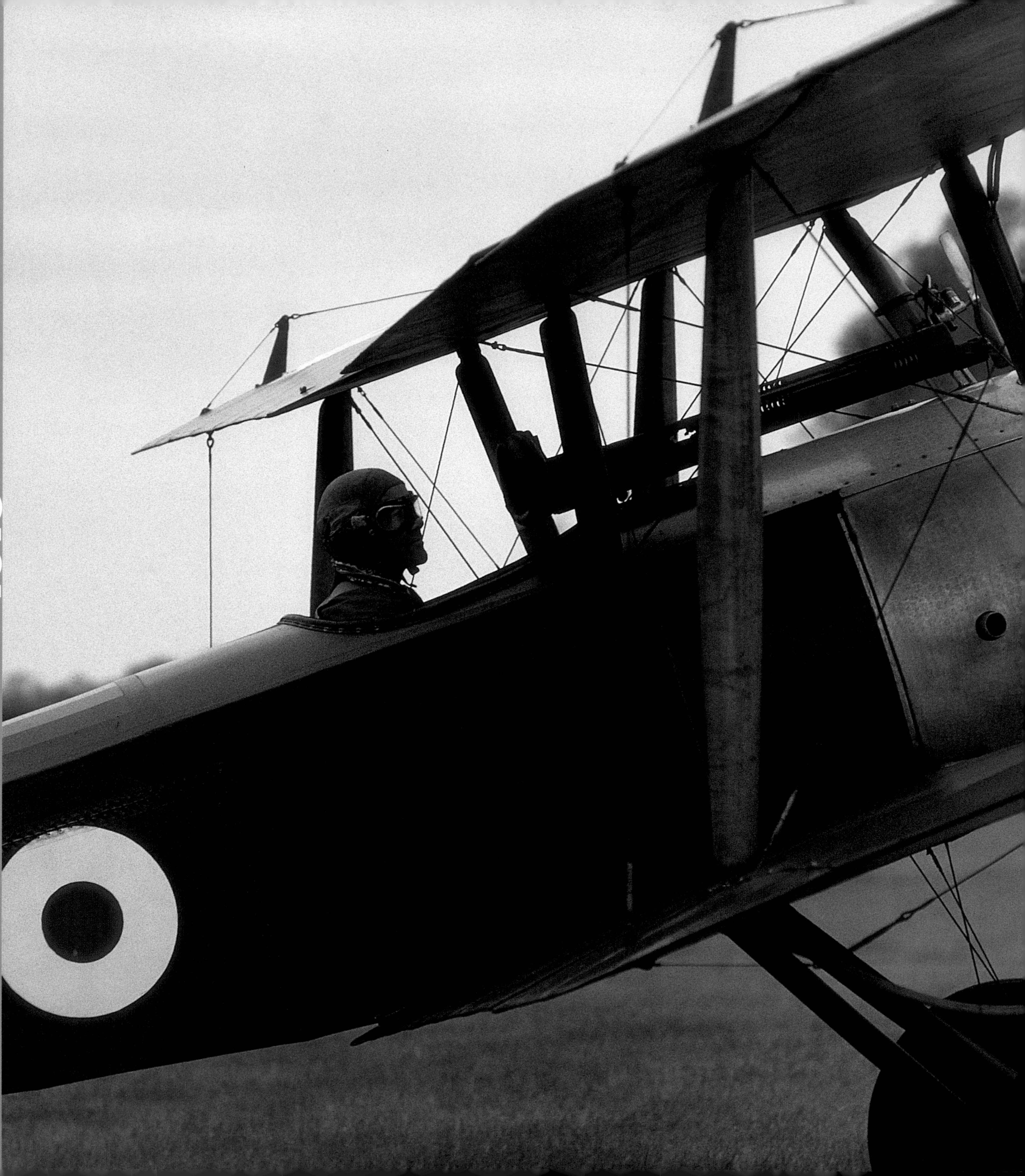

1915
Sopwith Types

Sir Thomas Sopwith lived through almost all of the first century of flight. He died at the age of 101 in 1989. But it was in 1915, at the age of 27, that he created the first of the line of planes that bore the brunt of combat for the British Royal Flying Corps in World War I. By this time his firm, started by the young but world famous flyer in 1912, had its "gang" together: Sopwith and R.G. Smith as chief designers, Harry Hawker in development and test piloting, and Fred Sigrist as engine designer. An earlier Sopwith plane, the Tabloid, had some success in the early days of the war, bombing German Zeppelin sheds in October 1914, but it was the "One-and-a-half strutter" Sopwith, built for the Admiralty in December 1915, that first gave British flyers a fast, sweet-flying, adaptable, two-place scout with a coherent armament: an offensive forward-firing gun and a ring-mounted gun for the observer's defense.

In swift succession came newer and better Sopwith fighters, each advancing in speed, power, and deadliness, yet each remaining a "pilot's airplane."

Entering service in 1916 was the "Pup," a masterpiece of harmonized control which, with its forward-firing machine gun, deserved most of the credit for ending the "Fokker Scourge" of 1916 when Fokker E.III monoplanes with synchronized guns wreaked havoc among Allied planes. There were 1,800 "Pups" built.

By 1917, Sopwith began production of the Camel, named for the hump in front of the pilot where the twin Vickers guns nestled. First for the Royal Navy, then the RFC (soon to become the Royal Air Force) the Camel earned its renown by disposing of 1,300 enemy airplanes. But gyroscopic forces from its short coupled rotary engine affected turning and diving in strange ways that could be dangerous to novice pilots.

The Snipe arrived in the summer of 1918. Arguably the best fighter of the war, it had little chance to prove itself as fighting ended in November. The redoubtable British ace Major Billy Barker won his Victoria Cross in a Snipe, and they became the standard RAF fighter after the Armistice, taking on the postwar bright silver finish and serving as late as 1927.

1916

1916
Albatros D.V

As the Battle of the Somme raged in the summer of 1916, a new and deadly shape took possesion of the skies above the trenches. A shark-like molded plywood fuselage and fin, tightly enclosed straight six Mercedes engine capped by a streamlined prop spinner, two synchronized guns; these were marks of the new predator: the Albatros D.I fighter. When combined with the more aggressive German tactics arising from the formation of "hunting squadrons" or Jastas, pioneered by the early German ace Oswald Boelke, Allied air forces suffered appalling losses through the end of the year.

Over time, certain flaws in the Albatros design grew evident. No more than 185 hp could be squeezed from the motor, even as French and British V-8 designs pushed toward 250 hp. An ill-advised sesquiplane wing design introduced in later marks might collapse in a dive. By summer of 1917, when the subject of our photos appeared, the Albatros was obsolescent. "Blue Max" medal-winner Hauptman Eduard Ritter von Schleich flew an Albatros D.V as commander of Jasta 21. This replica, flown at Rhinebeck for many years, carries his Bavarian lion medallion. The plane later received a black fuselage as von Schleich mourned the death of a comrade.

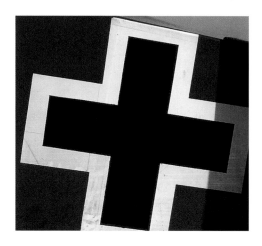

1917
Fokker Dr. I Triplane

Tiny, underpowered, badly constucted, hard to handle, yet for Germany the Fokker Triplane was for a while a wonder weapon. Even before he first flew the new "Dreidecker" fighter, Baron Manfred von Richtofen was telling his squadron mates about its qualities: "Climbs like an ape and as agile as the devil." He wanted

one, though it would be the death of him. On his first flight, September 7, 1917, he scored his sixtieth kill. All Richthofen's subsequent twenty victories up until his death on April 21, 1918, were won flying the Triplane, painted a glorious red, of course.

Anthony Fokker was happy to supply new machines, but German industry did not seem up to the task. Their 110 hp rotary engines, even though technologically obsolescent, could not be produced in quantity. Rotaries were scavenged from downed Allied craft. Furniture workers building the wooden wings were unskilled and slipshod. Fokker himself was almost jailed for treason as Dr.Is broke up in combat. The small number of triplanes reaching squadrons—about seven percent of all fighters in service—were grounded twice for wing failure. Even so, some of the greatest German aces could fly rings around most Allied ships in the Triplane.

1918
Royal Aircraft Factory
S.E. 5a

When the Allies began their big push in the summer of 1918, the principal British fighter planes were the Sopwith Camel and the S.E. 5a. Unglamorous, square-jawed and unstreamlined in appearance, under appreciated by some of her pilots, the S.E. got off to a slow start. When the first S.E. 5s arrived at the front in early 1917, they were almost universally disliked. A comment by leading ace Albert Ball is typical: "The S.E. 5 has turned out a dud." Even when equipped with a thirty percent more powerful 200 hp motor, and renamed the S.E. 5a, there were problems. Supplies of engines could not meet demand. Up to 400 complete planes sat at factories in January 1918, waiting for engines.

As supply problems were solved, more squadrons got the new 5a.

Another ace, James McCudden, summed up the qualities that now made the dowdy plane a winner: "Its great strength, its diving and zooming powers...far and away superior to the enemy machines of that period."

The Shuttleworth aircraft pictured is the last flying S.E. 5a left, survivor of a hazardous career with the Savage Skywriting Company in the twenties, now restored to her original serial number and finish.

1919
SPAD VII / XIII

After the Armistice was declared on November 11, 1918, the combatants rushed to divest themselves of anything to do with war. On airfields, great heaps of airplanes were made into bonfires. France, which had standardized on the SPAD XIIIc.1 as its main fighting aircraft, kept reduced quantities in service until 1923. About 400 went to the U.S. in 1919. They lingered on for a while in the impoverished U.S. Air Service, re-fitted with lower power American engines, which rendered them useless as fighters.

But when new, what fighters they had been! French ace Georges Guynemer called the SPAD his "Avion magique," his "flying machine gun" and flew it as if it had been custom-designed for him. Design credit goes to Louis Bechereau, the man resposible for the pre-war racing Deperdussins. That heritage shows in rudder shape and landing gear, but the smoothly cowled Hispano-Suiza motor and low-slung biplane wings give the SPAD a Gallic panache that the stodgy S.E. 5, which had the same engine, totally lacked. Brilliant markings only added to the effect. Illustrated here are designs carried by "Les Cignones"

(the Storks), as French aces were called, and by American ace Eddie Rickenbacker.

Other nations were not so quick to abandon the SPAD. Japan, as an emerging world power, gave military development a high priority, particularly in the air. In April 1919, license production began of the SPAD XIII for the Japanese Army.

**1920
Curtiss JN-4 Jenny**

It was the beginning of the Roaring Twenties and America had gone "Plane Crazy." One of the stars of that era would be the Jenny, as unglamorous a heroine as could be imagined, a cast-off, homely, gawky training plane from Curtiss, the JN-4D.

On the night of August 2, 1920, a white-painted Jenny flown by stunt pilot Omer Locklear caught the glow of searchlights as he began a spinning dive from 3,000 feet. Filming of the climactic scene of The Skywayman had begun. But Locklear, apparently blinded by the arclights, never pulled out of his dive, crashing the Jenny into an oilfield near Los Angeles. The funeral made headlines across the country.

Other less-spectacular barnstormers criss-crossed the country in those years. Jennys could be bought for a song from a war-weary government that had 8,000 to dispose of. The 90 hp OX-5 powerplant demanded work, but nothing that any garage mechanic couldn't handle. The Jenny's wide wings made for gentle flying with a couple of paying joyriders, and spread a welcome emergency roof over your bedroll at night. Jenny opened the door to women aviators as well, such as wing-walker Gladys Ingle and pilot Mabel Cody.

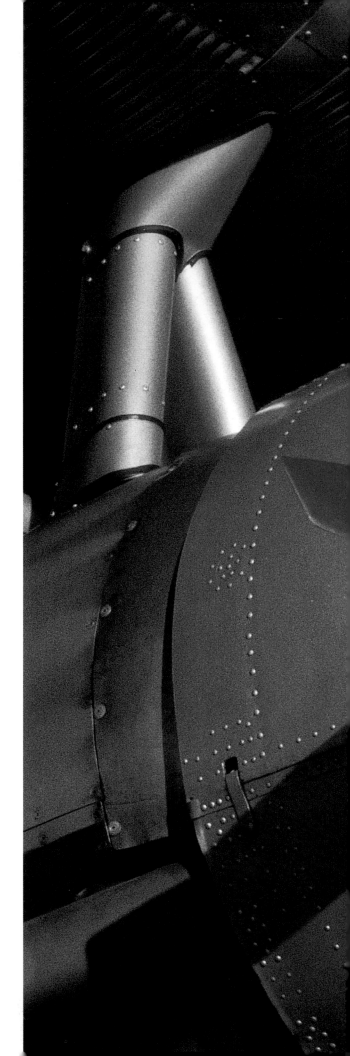

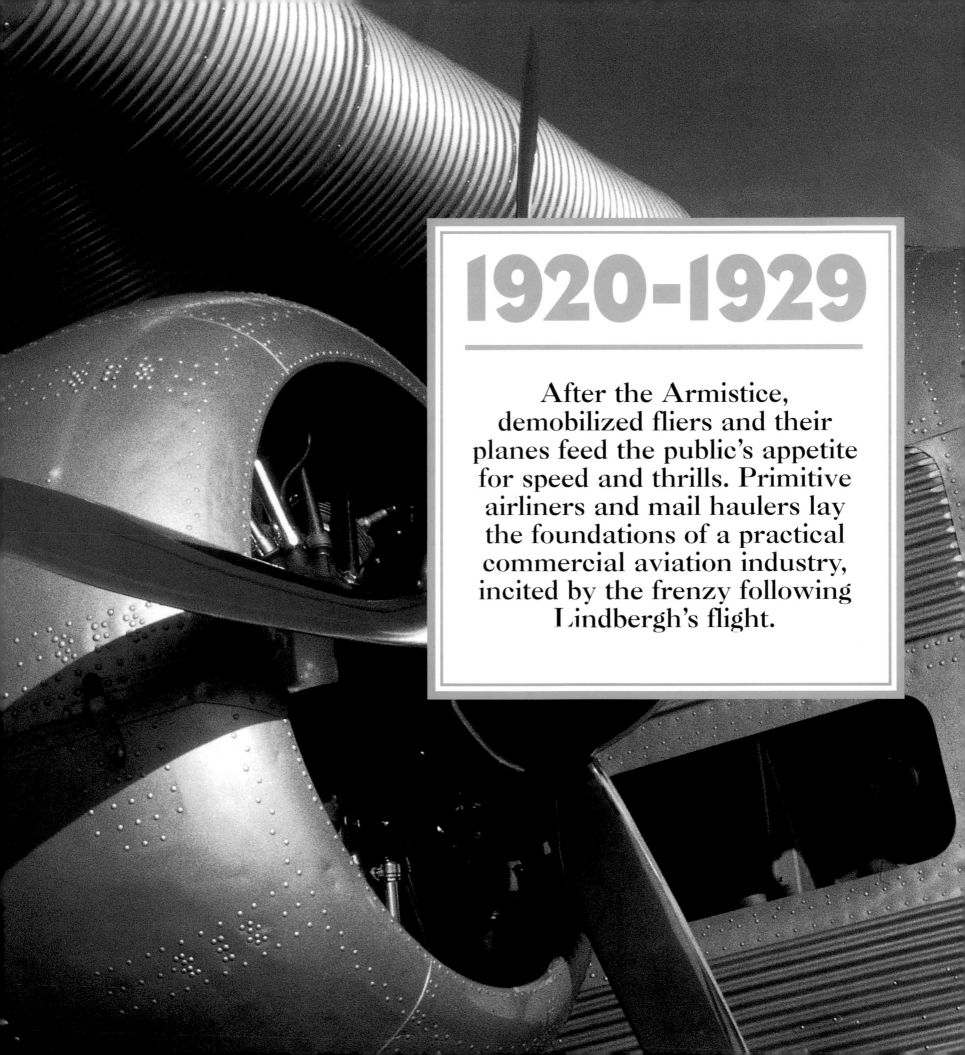

1920-1929

After the Armistice,
demobilized fliers and their
planes feed the public's appetite
for speed and thrills. Primitive
airliners and mail haulers lay
the foundations of a practical
commercial aviation industry,
incited by the frenzy following
Lindbergh's flight.

1921
Thomas-Morse S-4C Tommy

Another ex-warplane that could be had on-the-cheap in the early twenties was the Tommy. Smaller than the Jenny, the Thomas Morse S-4 scout had been designed in 1917 by a former Sopwith engineer as a pursuit trainer, and bore some resemblance to the Sopwith Tabloid. Although the military had taken delivery of almost 600 Tommys by 1918, they now felt that rotary-engined trainers were too hard to handle for low time students, so unloaded most as surplus.

Eagerly snatched up by would-be barnstormers, the Tommy became a gypsy trouper. The plane was nimble, fully aerobatic, and unlike the Jenny, ground handling was a one man job. Once the fire-prone Gnome engine was replaced by a French Le Rhone or even a Curtiss OX-5 V-8, the S-4 made a reliable stunt plane. With the equivalent of 200 planes worth of spare parts on the market, the Tommy was a tinkerer's dream. By 1921, conversions such as the two- and three-seat Yackey Sport were popular, and some of America's finest plane builders—men like Charles Meyers of Waco Aircraft and Jimmy Wedell of Wedell-Williams racer fame— first got their hands dirty doing conversions. The Tommy scout went on to a flashy movie career later in the twenties, most being reduced to matchwood for films such as *Wings* and *Dawn Patrol*.

1922
Bristol F.2B Fighter

In July 1922, the last wartime Bristol Fighters were recalled from Germany as the British Occupation Forces were withdrawn. The F.2B was a two-place fighter that could fight like a one-man scout. Large, but well-balanced and maneuverable, and with reserves of power, the key to her success was the back-to-back positioning of the crew, allowing instant communication and coordination.

The work of policing the Empire had scarcely begun for the "Brisfit," as she was later lovingly called. It was said that the sight of a formation of Bristols overhead could halt a tribal uprising in its tracks. In 1922, the far-flung squadrons of the RAF got many chances to prove this. In April, thirty-eight F.2Bs were expected to support army garrisons against tribal unrest over an area of 30,000 square miles of India. In Mesopotamia, or "Mespot" as RAF troops called it, Sheikh Mahmoud declared a "Jihad" against

the British in October. Brisfits raided his strongholds. Outside Constantinople that winter, followers of Attaturk besieged the city. Bristols flew from the aircraft carrier H.M.S. *Argus* (for the first time ever) to support the city's defenders at Gallipoli.

Some of these Bristols still had bullet hole patches from World War I. Supplies and parts were scarce, but the threadbare RAF got the job done and the veteran Brisfit went on to serve for ten more years.

1923
Junkers F.13

In 1919, weeks after the Armistice was signed, Professor Hugo Junkers, a visionary pioneer builder of all metal aircraft, started planning the construction of the first modern airliner. By 1923, one Junkers F-13 monoplane per week was leaving the production line at Dessau, Germany.

As passengers clambered over the thick corrugated wing, through the triangular door, and into the plush-lined cabin they surely recognized that this plane was like no other: no strutted biplane wings, no wires, a totally enclosed cabin—even seatbelts! With the merits of the plane itself—strong, durable, adaptable—and the financing deals provided by Junkers, it was no wonder they were employed worldwide: first through Europe, then South America and the Far East. About 320 were built in many different guises, some on floats serving the lakesides of Switzerland, some on skis in Finland, a few in the New Guinea gold fields. In 1920, the U.S. Post Office bought eight for use on its mail routes; one of them is pictured here, an American JL-6 now preserved in Paris.

So useful was the F-13 that production continued for nine more years, until 1932. Some remained in first line service until World War II. Varig, the airline of Brazil, was rumored to be flying a couple until 1948.

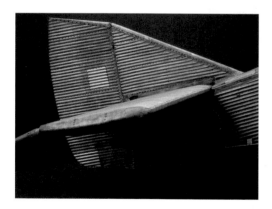

1924
Curtiss R3C-2 Racers

Guiding the design of the shapely Curtiss Racers was the principle: "If it looks right, it is right." As one of the first 200 mph aircraft, no surer guide existed to streamlining the curves of cowl and tailplane than the human eye. Aerodynamics then was an art of cut and try.

The first Curtiss racer, the CR-1, had flown in 1921. By 1923, a more sophisticated re-design using the world beating D-12 engine had clinched both the Pulitzer Race in the U.S. and the International Schneider seaplane race. So advanced were the R3C racers fielded by the U.S. Navy that competitors Britain, France, and Italy all bowed out of the 1924 Schneider. The U.S., as hosts of the race that year in Baltimore cancelled the event in a gesture of sportsmanship, to give the other nations' teams time to recoup.

Curtiss racers were not immune to disaster; roaring into a diving start at the October 1924 National Air Races, an R2C disentegrated after a wing strut collapsed. The month before, an older R-6 had crashed under similar circumstances. Diving starts were banned thereafter.

The R3C-2 shown here, as exhibited at the National Air and Space Museum in Washington, D.C., went on to win the 1925 Schneider Trophy, piloted by a young Jimmy Doolittle. Contrary to what might be guessed, these massive floats produced less drag than a wheeled landing gear.

45

1925
deHavilland Moths

Builder Geoffrey deHavilland collected moths as a hobby and named most of his sprightly creations—with their trademark parabolic rudder shape—after them. Shapely aircraft were important to deHavilland. He believed that "a designer must have much of the creative artist in him." In 1925, the first of the immortal Moths flew and, after numerous record flights and hundreds produced, a beautifully refined model named the D.H. 82 Tiger Moth appeared in 1931. It was a biplane sportplane and trainer without equal in the United Kingdom; 8,500 were built, and many are still flitting about today.

At about the same time as the Tiger, deHavilland was attempting to bring air travellers in out of the weather with a small enclosed monoplane, the D.H. 80 PussMoth. Although a series of crashes marred its introduction, a penchant for record setting assured its success, especially in Australia and New Zealand. There were 285 built.

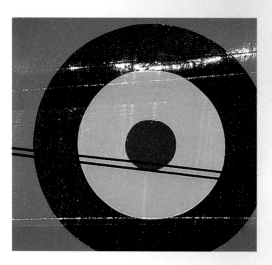

The year 1932 saw the introduction of the Fox Moth light transport, an expansion of the Tiger design with room for four passengers. A combination of economy and efficiency made the D.H. 83 Fox Moth very popular commercially, especially in the northern reaches of the British Isles, and about 100 were built. The plywood fuselage of the Fox presaged the construction of most future deHavilland aircraft, including the Albatross airliner and the wartime legend, the Mosquito fighter bomber.

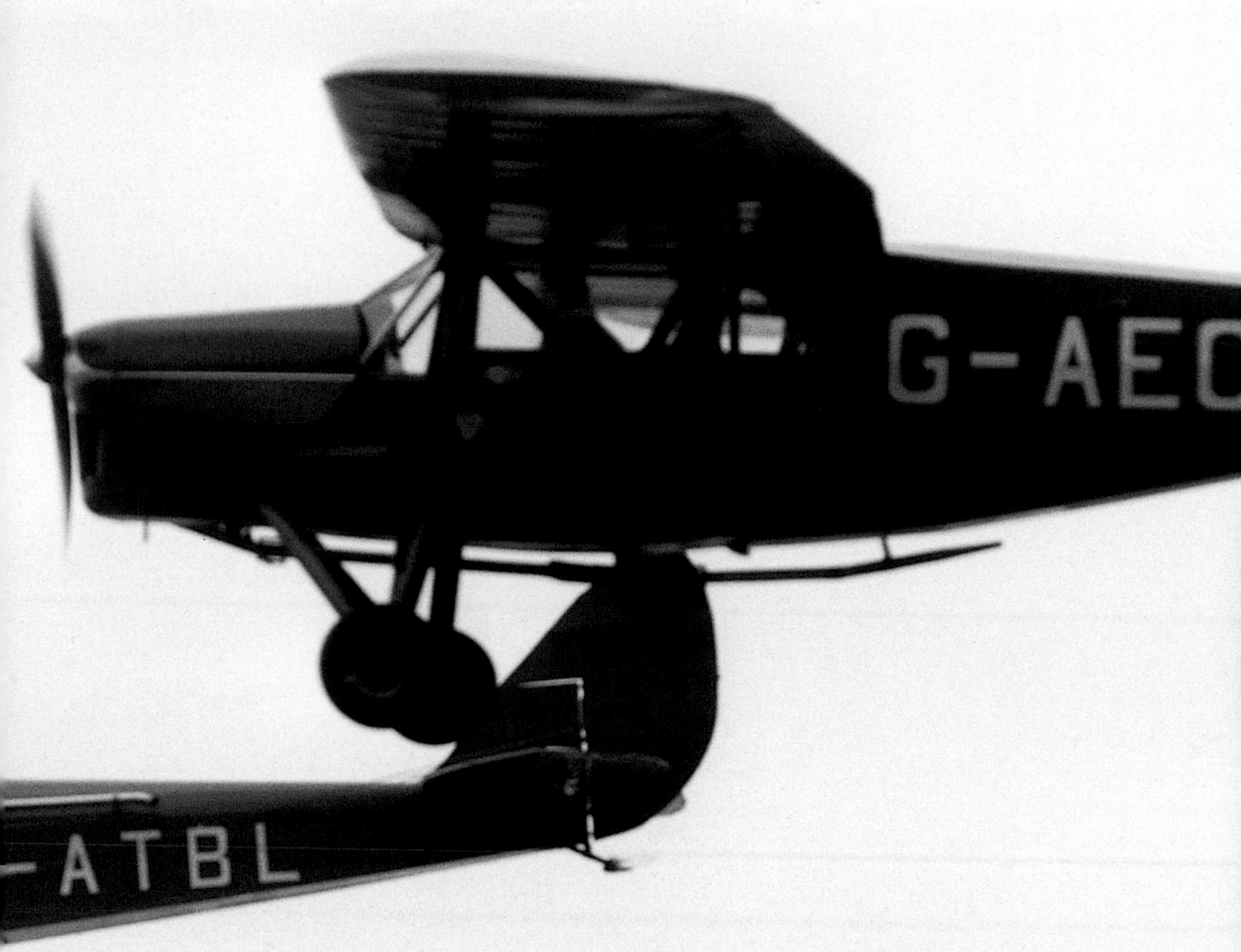
G-AEOA
ATBL

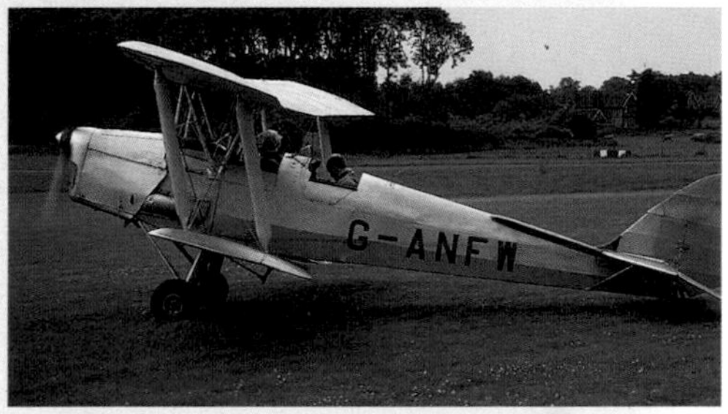
G-ANFW

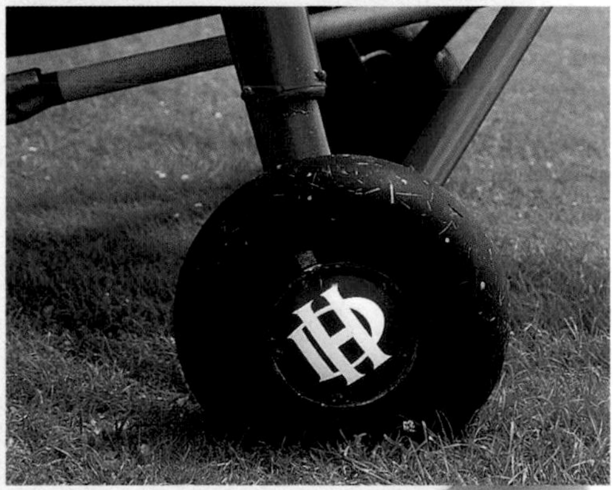

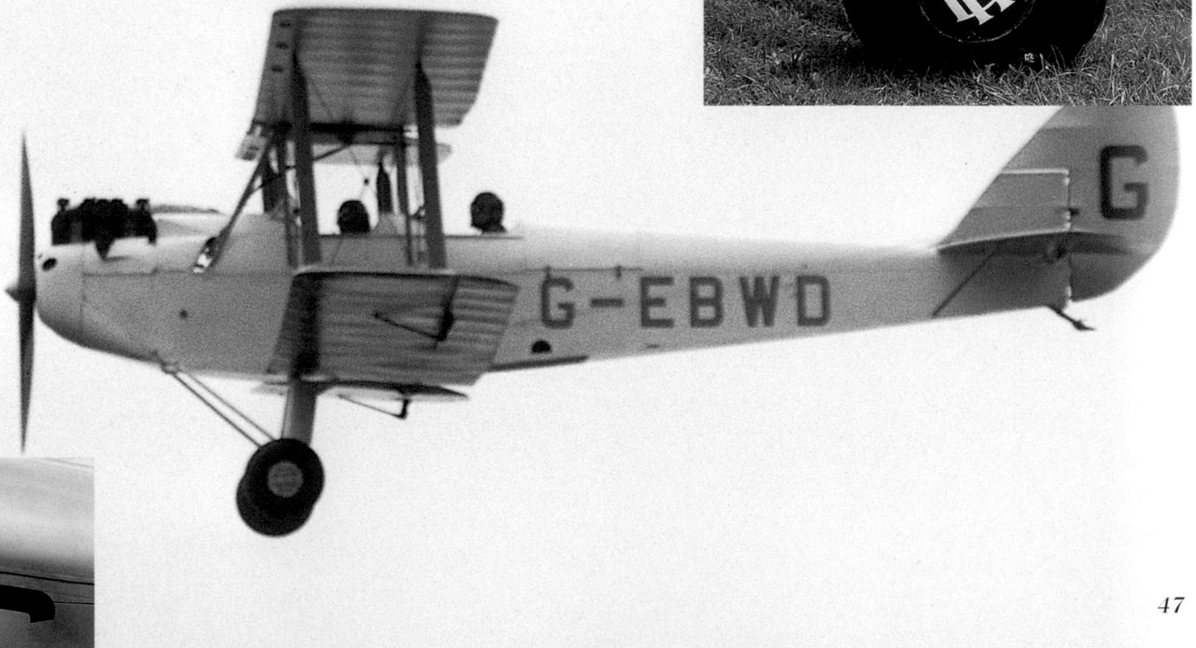
G
G-EBWD

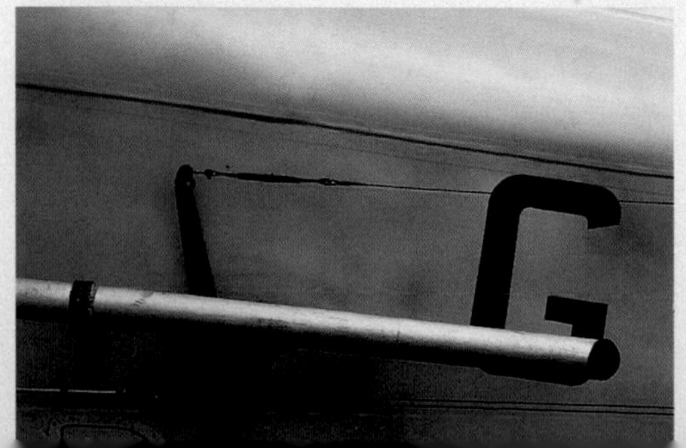
G

1926

1926
Ford Trimotor

Just as Henry Ford put America on wheels, he also went a long way toward giving the country wings as well. Ford enlisted William Bushnell Stout in his campaign to cash in on commercial air transport. Stout was a forward-thinking designer with new ideas in all-metal construction. His motto, "Simplicate and add lightness," has become the first commandment of

aero engineering. After a few abortive design attempts, the first true Ford Trimotor, the three-engined 4 A.T., took to the air on the 12th of June, 1926. The plane, nicknamed "The Tin Goose," borrowed its corrugated skin from Junkers and its general layout from Fokker's commercial craft. Since neither Stout nor Ford had much of an eye for beauty,

the Trimotors were not sleek streamliners; instead they communicated solidity, strength, and therefore safety to the public. This was just what was needed to get people accustomed to air travel.

By 1929, you could "fly" coast to coast on one ticket. Here's how: First a night train from New York to Columbus, Ohio, then by Trimotor to Oklahoma City. From there take the Santa Fe Railroad Sleeper to Clovis, New Mexico. Then another "Tin Goose" to Los Angeles. Total time: 48 hours. About a year later, you could travel by air all the way in just over 24 hours.

The Stout Bushmaster 2000 pictured here is a modernized version of the Ford and it still flies up at Owl's Head, Maine.

1927
Ryan Spirit of St. Louis

The most extraordinary thing about Charles Lindbergh's Atlantic-spanning plane was its very ordinariness; it looked typical of the new cabin monoplanes that were appearing on airfields around the country. Though the wings were long—46 feet—to boost range, the design was based on the small, four-place M-2 built by the then-unknown Ryan company. It was nothing like the multi-engine Fokker or Sikorsky heavyweights that Noel Davis and Admiral Byrd's crews had chosen. The engine seemed quite ordinary as well, a standard 220 hp Wright J-5, but the Whirlwind could run forever without a missed beat. The most unusual features were inside the plane, behind the burnished-but-windowless front cowl: a huge, 425-gallon fuel tank in back of which sat the single crewman.

Just one man to fly the 3,600-mile distance. This pilot looked pretty ordinary as well. He was just a kid really. Sure, he had lots of time in the air, barnstorming and flying the mail for the Army, but a nobody nonetheless. Still, "Slim" Lindbergh had organized, financed, and supervised the construction of his aircraft and single-handedly prepared every aspect of the record attempt. He then flew the 33 1/2-hour flight after almost two days without sleep.

And when he made it, Lindy's silver monoplane became for millions the image of the airplane, much as Bleriot's had when it crossed the English Channel in 1909, and its simple outline was reproduced in endless permutations in every medium and material. This full-sized 1928 B-1 sister ship of the Ryan NYP is held by the Cradle of Aviation Museum in Garden City, New York, sited near Lindbergh's Roosevelt Field departure point.

1928
Pitcairn PA-6 Mailwing

May 1, 1928 marked the beginning of mail flights on Civil Air Mail (CAM) Route 19, from New York to Atlanta, using the rakish new Pitcairn PA-5 Mailwing. The advent of lightweight, efficient radial engines finally put ex-military planes like the D.H.-4 and the Curtiss Jenny out of the airmail business. Walter Pitcairn, who built the Mailwing to fly his own mail routes,

found that the long-nosed biplane appealed to the sports pilot as well, and offered a two-place version for under $10,000.

As the depression deepened in the thirties, flying the mail was one of the few profitable growing businesses around. Pitcairn's routes on the east coast soon merged into Eastern Air

Transport, later renamed Eastern Air Lines. Pilots working for Pitcairn could make $6000 a year flying upwards of 120 hours a month, a princely salary indeed in those days.

This PA-6 Mailwing from 1928 carries original style air mail route markings and winged arrow logo.

51

1929
Monocoupe 90 Racer

The stylish, wasp-waisted Monocoupes got their speed almost as an afterthought, since designer Donald Luscombe wanted a small, civilized, efficient, personal plane that he could fly without helmet and goggles. He and legendary engineer Clayton Folkerts built the first Monocoupe in 1926. By 1929, new models such as the 65 hp

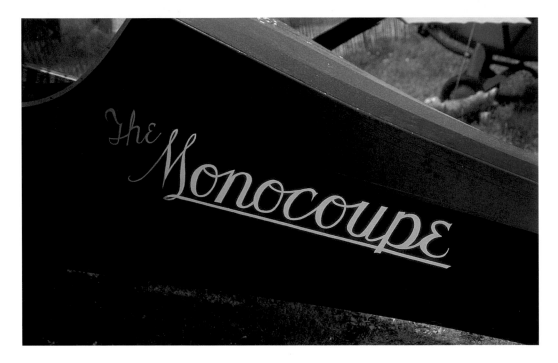

model 113 and the racing Monosports with 100 plus hp engines signaled a promising future for the plane.

The Monocoupe was comfortable, safe, and easy to handle, so why not sell it to women? Better yet, why not use women as sales reps or even as racing pilots? The Mono Aircraft Company did all of these things. They hired Amelia Earhart to do a month-long promotional tour in a company plane, appearing before women's groups around the country as order

books filled up. The Monocoupe, while never designed as a racer, was a superb competitor, especially in the later "Clipwing" 110 models. Women such as Helen McCloskey and Jackie Cochran set records in them. At the National Air Races in the summer of 1930, Monocoupes won eleven out of the fifteen races they entered.

The Monocoupe 90 set the pattern for today's high-wing, enclosed cabin Pipers and Cessnas.

1930
Great Lakes 2-T-1

Just one month before the October 1929 stock market crash, a tiny new aerobatic biplane, the Great Lakes Sport Trainer, was cavorting in the skies over the National Air Races. Powered by an American built version of the same four-cylinder, air-cooled Cirrus engine installed in the early deHavilland Moths, the Great Lakes proved slightly less successful.

After the 2-T-1's debut in March 1929, its upper wings were swept back to counteract tail heaviness. This, plus an advanced bi-curved wing section, gave the Great Lakes splendid aerobatic qualities, especially when flying inverted. The great Tex Rankin flew his Great Lakes on its back so much that he had his name painted upside-down along the side of the fuselage. His partner Dorothy Hester is said to have once flown 150 consecutive outside loops in her Great Lakes, surely an all-time record.

Even with the depression, the Great Lakes seemed to be flying high, placing third in the 1930 Cirrus Derby. But by late fall of that year, the company quietly went bust after building more than 200 planes. The few that still fly, such as this 1930 model flown by Cole Palen, are much beloved. Most, including Palen's, have been fitted with new engines.

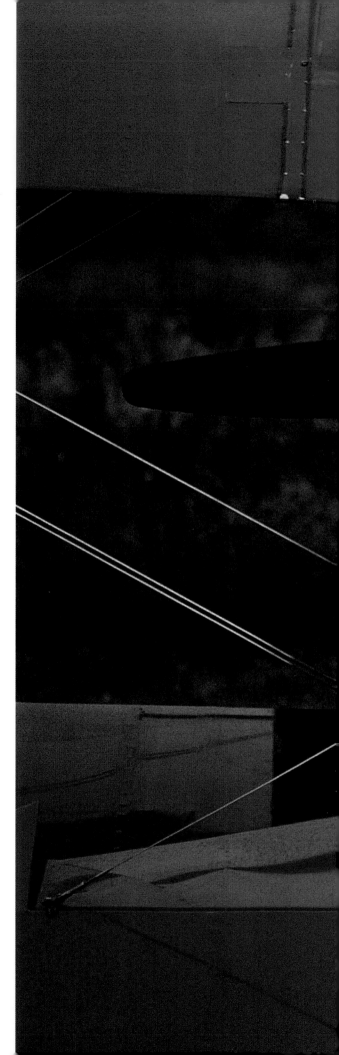

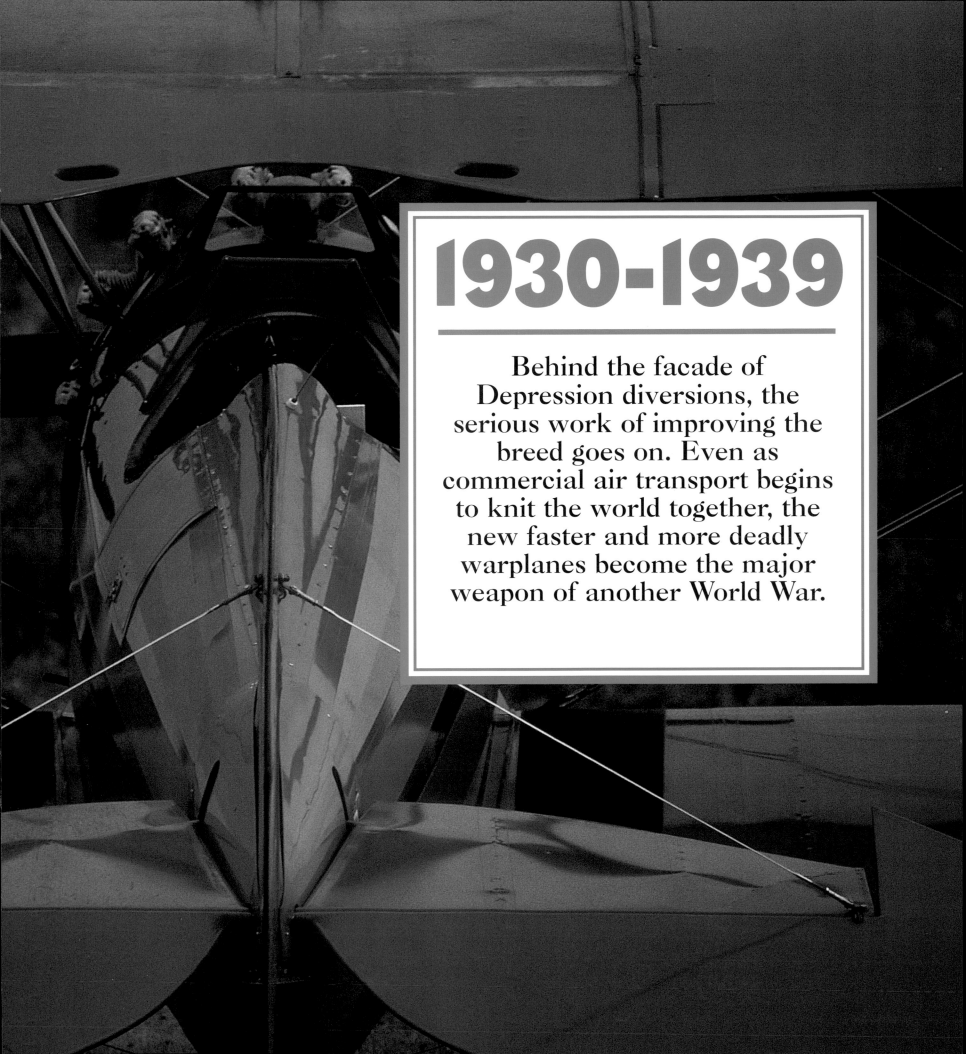

1930-1939

Behind the facade of Depression diversions, the serious work of improving the breed goes on. Even as commercial air transport begins to knit the world together, the new faster and more deadly warplanes become the major weapon of another World War.

1931
Supermarine S-5
Schneider Racer

England was very keen on racing in 1931. Even with the economic cutbacks of the depression, British sportsmen managed to garner speed records on land, sea, and in the air. The British also won outright possession of the Schneider Trophy after three straight wins of this bi-annual race by the magnificent Supermarine floatplane racers.

The plane shown in these photos is a flying replica, built for a British theme park, of the Supermarine S-5 that took the trophy in 1927. Based on lessons learned from Supermarine's gifted designer Reginald Mitchell's unsuccessful S-4 racer of 1925, the new all-metal S-5 was less curvaceous and lacked the cantilever wings that had given the S-4 its futuristic look, but were subject to flutter, in fact causing the S-4's crash.

While the 1929 race using brand new S-6 machines was hard fought, with the Italian Macchi M.52b coming in a close second, the 1931 race was basically a "walk-through." The winning S-6-B, however, was not a bogus champion. Its Rolls Royce type R engine was putting out 2550 hp by late September 1931, enabling the absolute air speed record to be raised to 407 mph. Mitchell and the RAF could justify the funds spent on these seemingly frivolous sporting events by applying the lessons learned in aerodynamics, metal working, and powerplant design to a warplane, possibly the most important fighter ever built, the Supermarine Spitfire.

1932

1932
Granville Brothers
Gee Bee R-2

The Thompson trophy! This deco bronze idol had been won the year before by a Gee Bee racer and builder "Granny" Granville wanted to take it again in 1932. His outré ideas on streamlining produced the tubby, teardrop-shaped R-2 and its brawnier sibling, the R-1, the plane that brought back the Thompson for Granny and his brothers—with some help from pilot Jimmy Doolittle. The planes were said to be killers, and they were—both craft later crashed, causing the death of their pilots.

In 1991, a full-sized, painstakingly accurate flying replica of the R-2 was built by Delmar Benjamin and Steve Wolf. Pilot Benjamin has proven that, given due respect, the R-2 can be

safely and excitingly flown. An airfoil-shaped fuselage makes "knife-edge" flying (with wings vertical) one of the Gee Bee's neater tricks. When Pete Miller, a ninety-year-old former drafts-man for Granville, heard the sound of the R-2 replica's first take off, he "laughed like a kid."

1934
Ryan S-T Sport Trainer

A perfect example of mid-thirties American optimism was *"Spirit of St. Louis"* builder Claude Ryan's re-entry into the aviation business with his 1934 Sport Trainer. The S-T's flashy, deco, Buck Rogers look made it an instant hit. By 1936, if you were a well-heeled sportsman, you could fly it away for $4500, lessons included.

The S-T gained a reputation as a "hot ship" with fliers raised on biplanes, but with its novel wing flaps, it was really quite docile. The U.S. Army, noting this, began ordering the S-T as the PT-16, their first monoplane primary trainer. As war loomed, more models were ordered, and as the Kinner-engined PT-22 "Recruit," more than a thousand served the Army and Navy until the end of hostilities. Many others wore the colors of air arms around the world, especially in Central and South America.

Still a favorite with private fliers who love the combination of open cockpit nostalgia, low-maintenance construction, and spirited performance, most have been restored to their gleaming polished metal pre-war finishes.

1933
Fairchild 22

A fair child indeed! This curvaceous parasol monoplane has had wheel pants and a close-fitting cowling with streamlined rocker arm covers installed. Its very deco paintwork was perhaps inspired by the colorful Beryloid paint company ads of 1928-1929, which used bird markings as a basis for airplane color schemes.

The Fairchild Camera Company found itself building aircraft for photo survey-ing work in the twenties, producing the sportier, less-utilitarian Model 22 in 1931 after acquiring the design from the Kreider Reisner Company. These first 22s, with their in-line four-cylinder engines, looked quite different from the 1933 model pictured, which has the later "Scarab" radial engine. In 1932, Fairchild brought an enclosed cabin up and under the parasol wing to produce the Model 24, which proved to be even more popular, serving during World War II and beyond as a light cargo ship.

1935
Waco Types

There were many Wacos; by some counts up to 110 different models of what were essentially variations on two themes: the open cockpit biplane and the cabin biplane. Our photos concentrate on the "open air" models.

In the late twenties, the Weaver Aircraft Co. of Troy, Ohio, later WACO, capitalized on the competitive prowess of its early models Nine and Ten to take a commanding lead in the private market, even while using the

problematic "O by Five" surplus engines. When superlative American radials like the Wright Whirlwind appeared, Waco consolidated its top position with the improved SO model, and in 1931, introduced a line of cabin model biplanes that sold well even during the depression. By 1935, a buyer could virtually customize his own plane to a desired price.

The muscular 1937 open cockpit UPF model caught the eye of the Army Air Corps; they bought hundreds as wartime trainers. These make up the

bulk of Wacos seen today. And the Waco name just will not die—in 1983, the Classic Aircraft Co. started license production of the old YMF "two-holer" and continues today with more than fifty sold. For the record, the name is pronounced "Wah-ko."

1936

RUSKIN AIR SERVICES

RUSKIN

1936
Douglas DC-3

On September 18, 1936, American Airlines began coast-to-coast Skysleeper service from Los Angeles to New York by selling their first ticket to none other than Shirley Temple. It is difficult now to envision the aura that surrounded the Douglas Sleeper Transport when it was introduced. Today it seems to us to have a slick kind of retro style, like an old Rolls Royce, but then it was the embodiment of the ideal of the thirties: streamlined, gleaming metal, a glamorous way to travel, safe but with just a tinge of adventure.

The impetus for the DST really came from C.R. Smith, the head of American Airlines. Wanting a sleeper plane or "Flying Pullman," he persuaded Donald Douglas to stretch

their successful DC-1/DC-2 design to accommodate fourteen berths. At first resistant, the Douglas staff began to realize that enlarging the plane led to huge improvements in the cost-per-passenger-mile equation. They quickly sketched out a twenty-one seater "day plane" which became the DC-3. Other airlines jumped to order the new Skyliner, and Douglas, unfettered by connections to any one airline, took on all comers. By 1939, up to ninety percent of air commerce world wide was flying in DC-3s.

The military was not slow to order transport versions, either, but once war began, the Douglas Skyliners, and the airways that had begun to connect the country coast to coast, vanished

overnight, as commercial planes were drafted from the airlines into military service. Ten thousand more DC-3s were specially built as C-47 Skytrains. But Americans believed that after the war the whole air transport system would come back, and with it the DC-3, only bigger and faster. By and large, that's just what happened. After the war, many manufacturers labored to design a DC-3 replacement, but it seems the only DC-3 replacement is—another DC-3. Many of them are working even now, some sixty years after they were built.

1937
Hawker Hind

A silver biplane on a close-clipped green, the perfect picture of the pre-war Royal Air Force. Preserved here in Afghan colors as part of the collection at Shuttleworth, England, the Hawker Hind light bomber was the last of a very photogenic series that included the Hart, Audax, and Osprey bombers and the Demon fighter. A closely related single-seater family included the Fury and Nimrod fighters.

The first of the family, the Hart, had flown in 1928 with a 500 hp Rolls Royce Kestrel engine under its close-fitting cowl. This winning combination made for a two-seat bomber that could outrun any British fighter. Dozens of permutations of engines and equipment were tried and built for the RAF until the Hind flew in 1934. It was basically an interim design to serve until the new monoplanes were available. At its peak in 1937, 500 Hinds served with Bomber Command and the Auxilliary Air Force, as well as several Commonwealth forces. In addition to the Afghan Hinds, Hawker sold models to Latvia, Yugoslavia, Persia, and Portugal. As obsolescence crept up, the RAF found use for the Hinds as trainers and target tugs, finally retiring them in 1942.

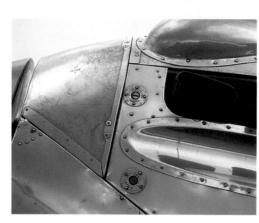

1938
Junkers Ju-52/3m

A squadron of unlikely looking bombers could be seen flying in loose formation over the Ebro river in October 1938 as the Spanish Civil War wound down to its inevitable Nationalist victory. Willed to Spanish crews by their previous owners, the German Condor Legion, the Junkers Ju-52—called the "Pava" or turkey by the Spaniards—made a slow and awkward bomber, but excelled in the role of transport. When Francisco Franco staged his coup attempt in 1936, a fleet of JUs lent by Fascist leader and ally Adolph Hitler air-lifted 10,000 Morroccan soldiers into Spain to back him.

As soon as the single-engined JU-52 became the three-engined JU-52/3m in 1932, it was immediately ordered by Lufthansa. Hundreds criss-crossed Europe until the outbreak of war. Then, in the green camoflage of the Luftwaffe, the Junkers took on any task assigned her; German fliers called her "Iron Annie" or "Tante (Auntie) Ju" with affection, and believed she could do anything. As ambulance plane, mine sweeper, glider tow-plane, paratroop drop ship, from the Mediterranean to Stalingrad, the Ju-52 was there until the final collapse. A few flying examples remain, such as this one, once owned by author Martin Caidin.

1939
Heinkel He-III

On September 1, 1939, when the German Blitzkrieg exploded into Poland, almost 300 Heinkel He-111 bombers targeted the major Polish cities. Coming direct from service in the Spanish Civil War, they went on to serve throughout World War II. Though they were fast, they were too lightweight to carry much of a bomb load or defensive armament.

This Heinkel is wearing camouflage in the "splinter pattern," an appropriate name evoking flying shell fragments and the angst of battle. It was a perfect background for the angular cross of the swastika. When Germany unveiled her hitherto secret Luftwaffe in the thirties in these dramatic colors, Hitler's aggressive intentions were made graphically clear.

The Heinkel 111, dating from 1935, is a menacing pug-nosed brute, even today. Dozens of camouflaged Heinkels lined the airfield in Madrid, Spain, in the mid-sixties—still in first line service! In 1969, a film company leased a batch for use in the movie *"The Battle of Britain"*. This one, performing at an air show on Long Island, New York, is a survivor of those planes, a Spanish-built variant with British Merlin engines.

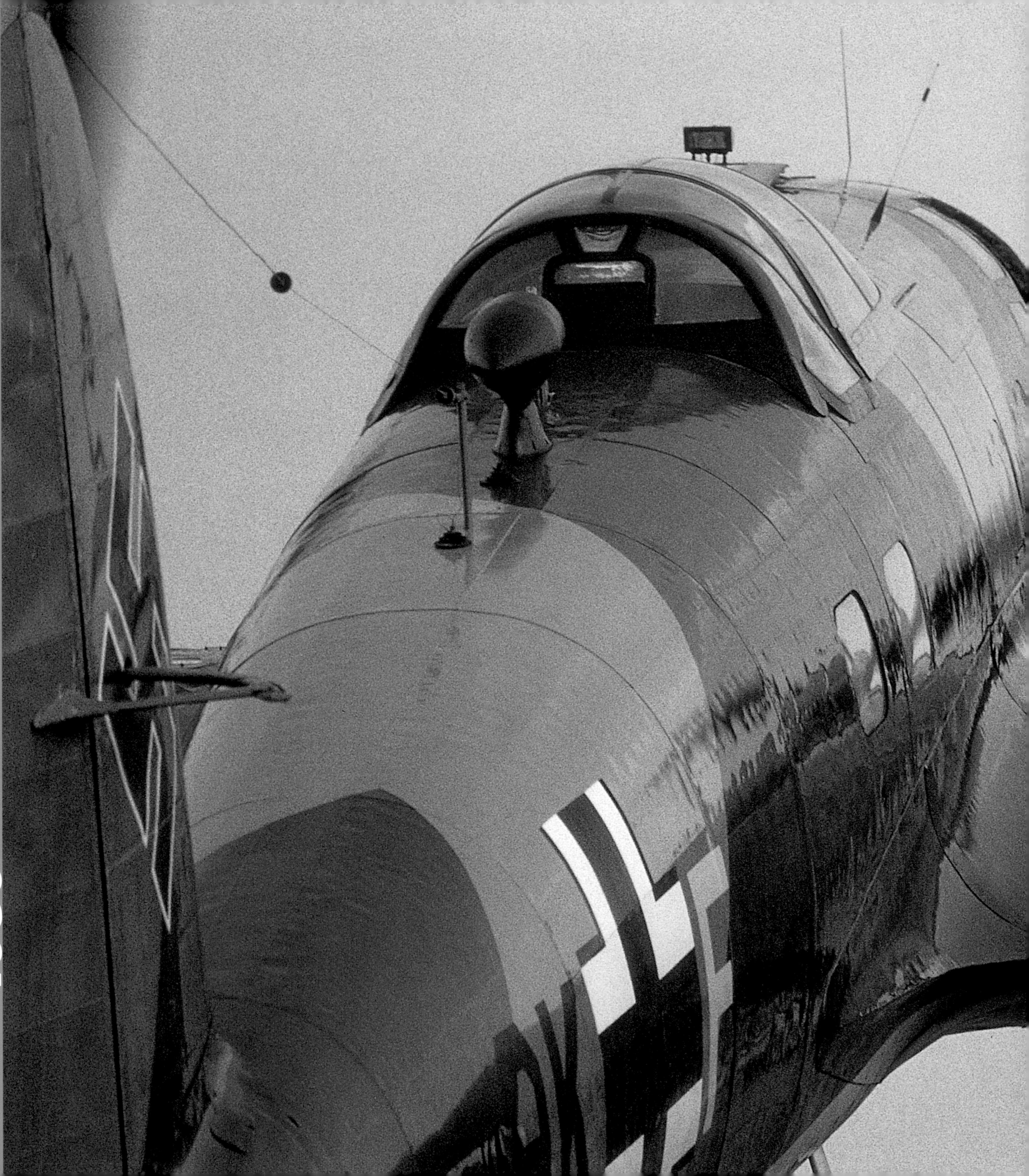

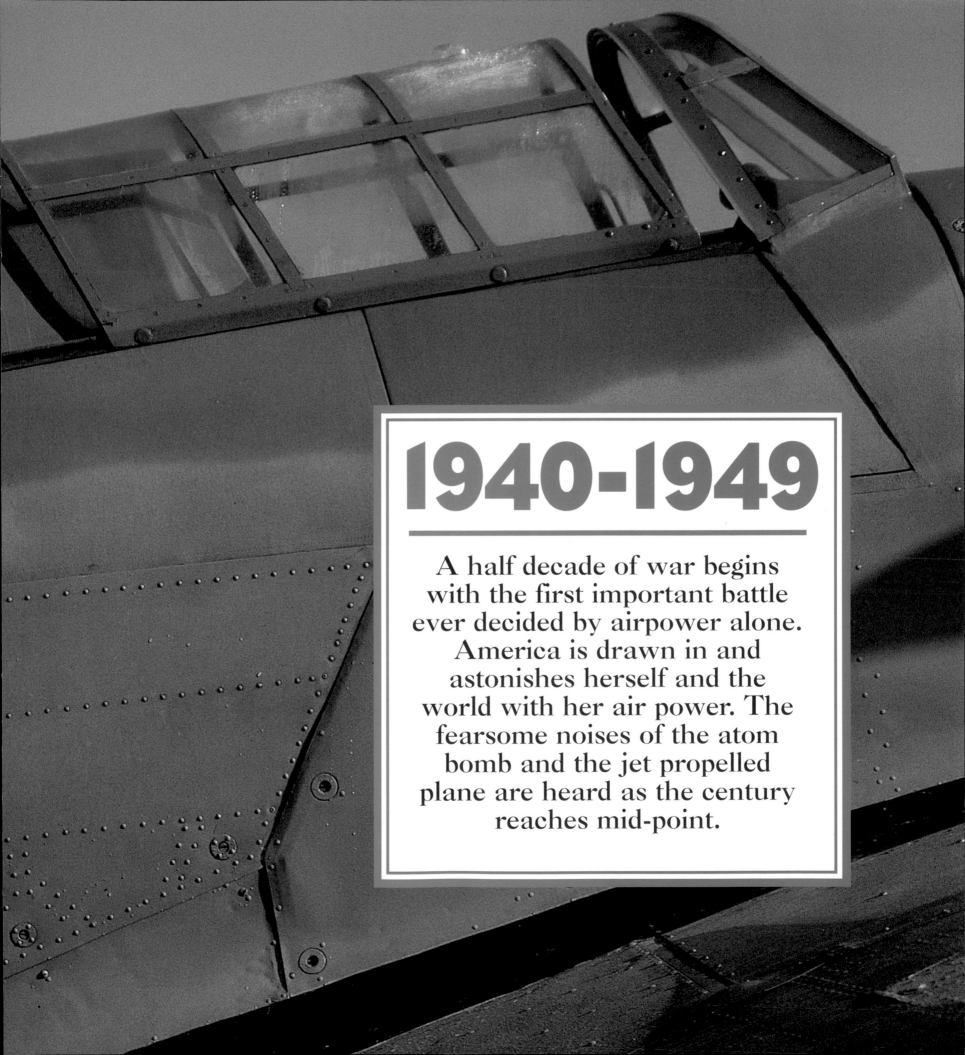

1940-1949

A half decade of war begins with the first important battle ever decided by airpower alone. America is drawn in and astonishes herself and the world with her air power. The fearsome noises of the atom bomb and the jet propelled plane are heard as the century reaches mid-point.

1940

The Hawker Hurricane and Supermarine Spitfire

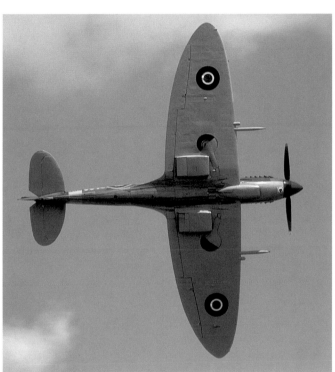

the hearts and minds of the English people. The RAF maintains a restored Spitfire and Hurricane in flying condition. They make appearances at airshows around the country.

A flash of those unmistakable elliptical wings and the understated growl of the Merlin engine— immediately you know it's a Spitfire. Slim and aristocratic, though hardly bloodless, the Spitfire was a sensuous design. It looked more like a racer than a warplane. In fact, its designer, Reginald Mitchell, built upon his Schneider Cup-winning floatplanes in designing the Spit. Though the wing's shape was aerodynamically derived, the ellipse became a motif for the entire craft. From nose to canopy, gun fairings to tail, all shapes and surfaces reflect the natural streamline shape of the ellipse. This machine's greatest power is not as a weapon, but in its ability to touch something deep within us and stir the imagination.

Never as dashing in the public eye as the rapier-like Spitfire, the Hawker Hurricane "did its bit." It

When dusk comes over the towns of southeast England and your eye is drawn to the sky, it is easy to see again the lines of German bombers; Heinkels and Dorniers, some flown from bases less than 100 miles away. First they came by day, then, unable to sustain the losses, by night—night after night of the Blitz. But attacking London rather than air bases was a fatal German error, as it allowed the Royal Air Force to rebuild and rest. It was a chancy thing, but the RAF won the Battle of Britain.

The Battle of Britain, fought in the summer of 1940, is still very much in

had the same engine, and same eight guns as the Spit, but its fabric-covered fuselage, heavy construction, thick wings, and boxy lines were from an earlier generation. So while the Spitfire went for the fighters on an interception during the Battle of Britain, the Hurricane took on the bombers. More planes fell to the Hurri's guns than to the Spit's, but by war's end they were all out to pasture and only two Hurricanes survive today. We were lucky to catch this Hurricane while it still flew. She was destroyed in a fire in Canada a few years ago.

73

1941
Mitsubishi A6M Zero/
Curtiss P-40

"Remember Pearl Harbor!" was the cry fifty-five years ago and there are a bunch of wild Texans who certainly do. The Confederate Air Force, a volunteer group who try to keep World War II planes flying, every year stages a re-enactment of the Pearl Harbor attack using these replicas of Japanese warplanes.

The dashing but overmatched Curtiss P-40 Warhawk, lazing in the morning sun, could lull us back to that sleepy Sunday morning in Hawaii on December 7, 1941. The day of the attack, eighty Zeroes from six carriers hammered Pearl in two waves along

with hundreds of dive and torpedo bombers. More than 200 U.S. aircraft were destroyed, most on the ground.

The designer of the Zero, Jiro Horikoshi, worked to create a beautiful plane, as nimble as a biplane,

yet with modern 300 mph speed. In doing so, he gave up a large margin of structural safety and pilot protection. Though American fliers were at first dumfounded by the Zero's perfor- mance at Pearl Harbor and other early battles in the Pacific, the advent of stronger, faster U.S. fighters such as the Hellcat and Corsair eventually shifted even the more advanced models of the A6M to the defensive. Of 10,000 Zeroes produced, many were sacrificed in the last reckless kamikaze attacks of 1945.

1942
North American B-25 Mitchell

This is a lethal weapon. Nothing is hidden here—every line expresses a death dealing efficiency. When President Roosevelt and Jimmy Doolittle wanted to take the war to the Japanese in April 1942, only the B-25 was small, powerful, and long ranged enough to fly from the deck of a carrier and bomb Tokyo, 700 miles away. Sixteen planes launched from the USS *"Hornet"* on the morning of April 18th; all hit targets in and around Tokyo, all but one eventually crashed in China. But the raid was a success: although damage on the ground was slight, the Japanese now had to devote serious resources to air defence. Back at home the boost to U.S. morale was incalculable.

The British used the Mitchell (as they named it) in every theater of war. Most wore camouflage of green or sand; the ones shown here were in the sinister black of night intruders. The Army Air Force found that a glossy black gave greater protection from searchlights: it produced starlike high-lights and didn't "pop out" against the night sky as a matte black plane would.

Easy to maintain, easy to fly, the B-25 made the postwar transition to business flying, and many are still airworthy today. But no matter how much they are gussied up, that purposeful warlike look remains.

1943
North American
P-51 Mustang

The P-51 Mustang was called the Cadillac of the air by novelist J. G. Ballard in his autobiographical *"Empire of the Sun"*. No other World War II plane better demonstrated America's ability to produce the right machine at the right time. Designed on a dare by North American's Dutch Kindelberger, who resented being told to build Curtiss P-40's, the first P-51 had the look but not the engine. It was the British who showed that a Merlin engine with twenty-five percent more power than the disappointing GM Allison motor could produce a world beater— 400 mph with ease, 2000-mile range, and the agility of its equine namesake.

On December 13, 1943, Mustangs with droptanks began escorting bombers by daylight. Now the American heavies had "little friends" all the way in and all the way back from their targets. Mustangs could handle anything the Reich could throw at it, including the new Me-262 jets, if caught at the right moment. In addition to long-range escort, Mustangs flew ground attack and interception, and more than 15,000 appeared in every theater of the war.

In its detail design, the Mustang showed economy and common sense. Streamlined to 1945 state-of-the-art, their mechanical durability enables hundreds of Mustangs to not merely survive but continue to thrive. Long after service in the Korean Conflict, The Mustang found a new battleground on the race course in Reno, Nevada. There, even today, the Mustang is still the odds-on favorite.

1944
Boeing B-17
Flying Fortress

When the Boeing Flying Fortress first appeared in 1935, five or six hand-held machine guns seemed fortress enough. By the time the B-17 entered combat in 1942, British bombers carried two to four guns in power turrets front and rear, above and below, and they were being stalked by German fighters with 20- and 30mm explosive-

These restored examples show the scramble for places to mount guns that continued throughout the European campaign. Ultimately, sheer numbers, rigid formation discipline, and the bravery of their crews were the Fortresses' best defense. The B-17s that are still airworthy today require enormous effort to keep them flying and their sole purpose, aside from thrilling those who see them and

shelled cannon. Even with near calamitous losses early in the war, American morale remained high and crews kept their minds firmly on other things, such as the "lucky" nose art painted on the sides of their planes. To make daylight bombing really viable, it took long-legged escort fighters like the Mustang. Bomber crews were always glad to see their "little friends."

fly in them, is as a memorial.
These beautiful machines and the
destruction they both caused and
endured, helped kill the myth of the
"purity of flight."

1945
Boeing B-29 Superfortress

Light years ahead of anything the Japanese had, the so-called hemisphere bomber concept, which culminated in the B-29 Superfortress, began with Boeing design studies in 1938. When General Hap Arnold demanded a 400-mph, 5,000-mile range bomber for the Army Air Corps in 1940, Boeing was ready. The first B-29 flew less than two years later, a truly miraculous feat considering the Superfortress used new engines, a new pressurized fuselage design, and revolutionary computerized remote-controlled guns.

Just the sheer size of the thing brought major problems. Huge factories went up, and giant bases were carved out of Pacific atolls and in China. Though the B-29 was designed as a high altitude bomber, General Curtis LeMay's innovative strategy was to go in at low level with incendiaries and burn the heart out of the Empire of Nippon. When the nuclear spawn of the Manhattan Project arrived, B-29s of the top-secret 509th Bomb Group delivered the coup-de-grace. Pictured is the the twenty kiloton Fat Man bomb that leveled Nagasaki, ending the war with a mushroom cloud exclamation point.

1946
Ercoupe / Piper Cub

When victory came, we would all have an Ercoupe like this one or a Luscombe Silvaire in our garage. Hundreds of magazine ads prepared American consumers for the postwar world of flying down to New Orleans for gumbo or buying a new Piper Cub in Macy's department store. By 1946, the sleek metallic realm of flight took up where it had left off five years before with hardly a stutter and, by 1947, thirty-thousand light planes left

the factories. Typical of those times was the 1946 Chicago Christmas parade in which Santa Claus used an Ercoupe for his sled.

The all-metal, twin-tailed Ercoupe had simplified controls so it would handle more like a car. This had its downside, since the Ercoupe's lack of separate rudder controls made it sluggish and unresponsive when compared to conventional planes.

But many young veteran pilots wanted nothing to do with flying. The new planes were overpriced, out of reach of newlywed ex-G.I.'s. Although private flying eventually grew more important in business and in remote areas, the air highways predicted by futurists never materialized. What has endured for these fifty years is the ageless Piper or Cessna on a grassy field puttering out for a day trip or joy ride.

1947
North American
T-6 Texan/Harvard

It was a teenager's wartime dream come true: flying high in a T-6 trainer, the next best thing to a real fighter plane. Fifteen thousand flew the bumps and circuits, taught formation flying and the basics of dogfighting to the hundreds of thousands of kids who aspired to Mustangs and Lightnings. Since 500 hp could be a handful, these advanced trainers, called "Texans" by the Army or "Harvards" by the Brits were built to take it—they were all metal throughout.

The North American AT-6 Texan dated from a 1935 design called the NA-16. The British "Harvard" appeared in 1938. Actually produced until 1954 in Canada, these planes were part of almost every nation's training course; some even saw combat. After peace came, they were put to every conceivable use: skywriting, racing, crop dusting, movie stand-ins for other planes, and in 1947, when the U.S. Air Force became a separate branch of service, the T-6 was still a mainstay, teaching future jet jockeys some humility. Just a few years later, in Korea, T-6's found a new identity as "Mosquitos"—forward air controllers—directing attack planes in the battle zone.

Hundreds of them are still flying today—and why not? They're great fun—and loud too!

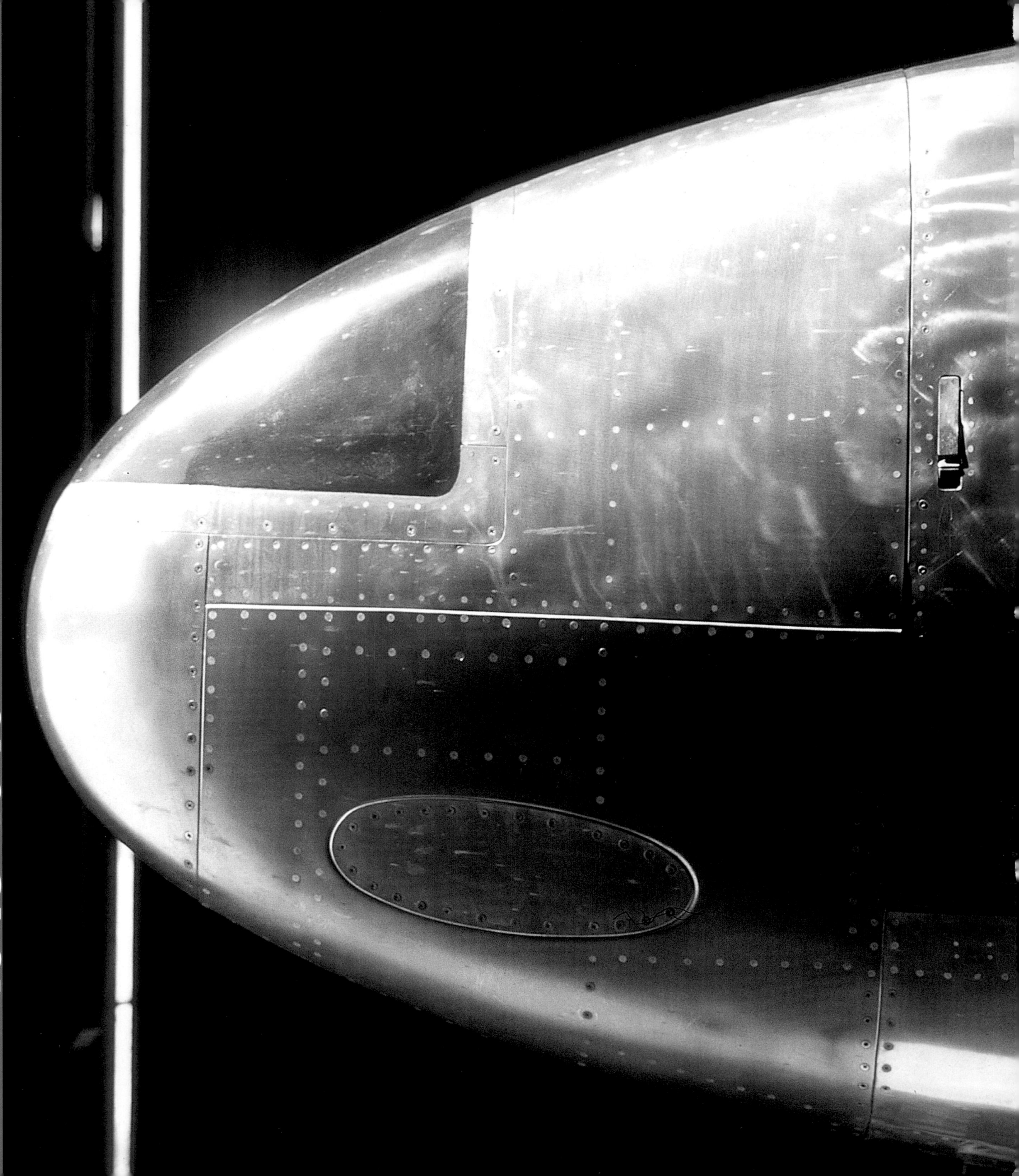

1948 -1949

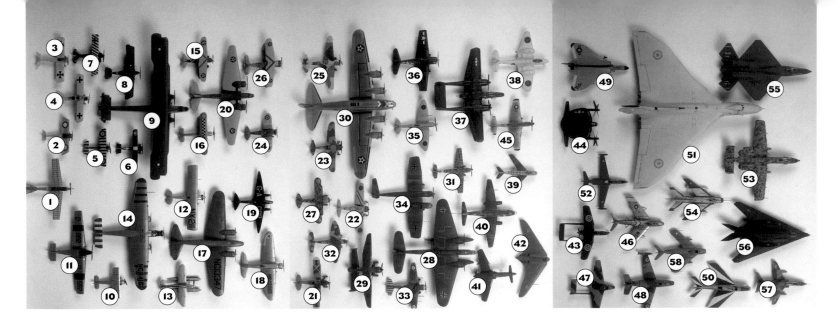

Key to Miniature Aircraft Pictured in Gatefold

Aircraft are shown in rough chronological order, running from left to right. Fourteen of the aircraft illustrated here are described in the text and shown in boldface in this key, but most of the 58 planes shown were chosen to illustrate interesting camouflage schemes or unusual design features. The date given is the year the airplane flew in the colors and markings shown, not the year of the plane's first flight. The models are built to a constant 1/72nd scale but are shown on these pages at approximately one-third that size. Models constructed by Frank D. Sullivan

1.	**Levasseur Antoinette VII**	France	1908	Racing machine
2.	Morane Type N Bullet	France	1915	Russian Air Service 19th Squadron
3.	Fokker E-III Eindecker	Germany	1915	Standard early War markings
4.	Roland C-2 Walfisch	Germany	1916	Special "fish" markings
5.	**Sopwith Pup**	GB	1917	Capt. Foote, Gosport Training School
6.	Sopwith Triplane	GB	1917	Flt LT Munro's "Dixie" 8th Sq. RNAS
7.	Fokker D VII	Germany	1918	Ace Ernst Udet's Plane
8.	Hannover CL-IIIA	Germany	1918	Shot down by US ace Rickenbacker
9.	Handley Page 0/400 "Langley"	USA	1918	American version of British plane
10.	Dayton Wright RB-1	USA	1920	Gordon Bennet Racer
11.	**Junkers F.13**	Germany	1925	Lufthansa German Air Line
12..	**Ryan Spirit of St. Louis**	USA	1927	Lindbergh's New York to Paris plane
13.	**Supermarine S.6B**	GB	1931	Schneider Winner Lt.Boothman
14.	**Ford 5-AT Trimotor**	USA	1931	Pan Am Airlines in Peru
15.	Curtiss P-6E Hawk	USA	1932	94th Squadron, US Army
16.	Hawker Fury I	GB	1932	34 Squadron, RAF
17.	Boeing 247D	USA	1934	United Air Lines
18.	Northrop Gamma "Skychief"	USA	1934	Texaco record setter
19.	Dehavilland DH 88 Comet	GB	1934	GB to Australia racer"Black Magic"
20.	Martin B-10 B	USA	1937	US Army 31st Bomb Squadron
21.	Heinkel He 51b-1	Germany	1937	German Condor Legion in Spain
22.	Nakajima KI 27A Nate	Japan	1939	Lt Col Kato 1st Gp Japan's AAF
23.	PZL P-11c Jedenastka	Poland	1939	Markings during German invasion
24.	Boeing P-26C Peashooter	USA	1939	6th Sq.Ldr.,US Army Air Corps
25.	Curtiss P-36A Mohawk	USA	1939	27th Squadron War Games paint
26.	Curtiss SBC-4 Helldiver	USA	1940	Naval Reserve Sq."Golden Gators"
27.	Fiat CR 42 Falco	Italy	1940	Italian AF, Belgium, Battle of Britain
28.	Heinkel He-115B-1	Germany	1940	German mine layer Battle of Britain
29.	Westland P.12 Wendover	GB	1941	Tandem wing prototype
30.	**Boeing B-17C Fortress**	USA	1941	88th Obs Sq, Pre WWII colors
31.	Messershmitt Bf.109E-4 Emil	Germany	1941	African markings JG 27
32.	Heinkel He-112B-1	Germany	1942	Span. Nationalists, Melilla, Morocco
33.	M.Bloch MB 152c.1	France	1942	Vichy Air Force colors
34.	Blohm & Voss BV 141B-0	Germany	1942	Prototype "assymetrical" plane
35.	**Supermarine Spitfire VII**	GB	1944	Photo Recon Spitfire, D-Day
36.	Grumman F6F-5 Hellcat	USA	1944	VF-27 squadron on Carrier Princeton
37.	Northrop P-61B Black Widow	USA	1945	Night fighter made last WWII Kill
38.	Gloster Meteor F.Mk.3	GB	1945	616 Squadron winter camouflage
39.	Messerschmiitt P-1101	Germany	1945	Prototype swept wing jet, not flown
40.	Arado AR 234B-2	Germany	1945	Jet bomber captured by Allies
41.	Kyushu J7W-1Shinden	Japan	1945	Prototype "canard" fighter
42.	Gotha GO-229 A-0	Germany	1945	Prototype flying wing never flew
43.	Saab J-21A	Sweden	1948	2nd Squadron Swedish Air Force
44.	Vought XF5U-1Flapjack	USA	1948	1st prototype, never flown
45.	**N. American P-51 Mustang**	USA	1950	Lt Glessner 12th FBS Korea
46.	**N. American F-86E Sabre**	USA	1953	Col Royal Baker 336 Sq Korea
47.	DeHavilland FB.52 Vampire	GB	1956	Iraqi Air Force
48.	Dassault Ouragan	France	1956	Israeli AF, 113 Squadron, Suez
49.	DouglasF4D-1 Skyray	USA	1959	Navy fighter with NORAD
50.	RepublicF-84F Thunderstreak	USA	1960	"Getti Tonanti" aerobatic team, Italy
51.	Avro Vulcan B2A	GB	1964	617 Sq RAF "V-Bomber"
52.	**Fouga CM-170 Magister**	France	1970	"Les Diables Rouges", Belgian AF
53.	**Fairchild A-10A "Warthog"**	USA	1978	Experimental camouflage USAF
54.	**MiG-19(F-6) Fantan**	China	1981	Pakistan AF Aerobatic Squadron
55.	Northrop YF-23Black Widow II	USA	1991	Prototype lost out to F-22
56.	**Lockheed F-117 Nighthawk**	USA	1991	Col Tolin, 37 TFW, Gulf War
57.	Hawker SiddelyHawk Mk. 61	GB	1991	Dubai Air Force, Gulf War
58.	**MiG-17 Fresco A**	USSR	1993	Somalian Air Force

1948
The Lockheed T-33

Serious problems surfaced as the U.S. Air Force began switching to new jet fighters such as the sleek Lockheed F-80 Shooting Star. Inexperienced pilots were slow to adapt to turbine engines' tricky throttle responses. Even the nation's top wartime ace, Major Richard Bong was killed test flying a new P-80. (P for Pursuit gave way to F for Fighter in 1948.)

By grafting a two-foot section onto the fuselage of the F-80 and extending its Plexiglas canopy, the two-seat TF-80 was created to ease transition training. The Lockheed TF-80, soon to be re-designated T-33, first flew on March 22, 1948, and with its longer fuselage proved faster than its parent. Never officially named, the plane was later universally known as the "T-Bird." The Air Force instantly ordered 128, to be converted from fighters on order. Lockheed went on to build almost 6,000 T-Birds. Though the F-80 had been our first successful

jet fighter, with 100,000 combat sorties flown in Korea, it was as the "T-Bird" that the plane became immortal. Virtually every non-communist country's air force used them. In fact, the T-33 is the only first-generation jet design that is still doing useful work today, more than half a century after the first of its breed flew in 1944.

1949
Republic F-84 Thunderjet

These new 600 mph Thunderjets looked like the shape of things to come for the U.S. Air Force: sleek, simple, with huge air-gulping intakes to feed their 5,000-pound thrust jet engines. In September 1946, a new F-84 set a

speed record of 611 mph. But all was not well with the Thunderjet. The plane was overweight and underpowered, some systems—such as the new radar gunsight—were overly complex, and exterior skin wrinkling hinted at possible structural deficiency.

By 1949, Republic Aviation was on the brink of bankruptcy, faced with Air Force cancellation of hundreds of F-84s. Luckily, the new F-84E model with uprated engines seemed to solve most problems. The 27th Fighter Escort Wing began to iron out the kinks just in time, as every available plane was scrambled to Korea after the North Koreans invaded on June 25, 1950. Here, though outclassed as interceptors against the swept wing Mig-15, the F-84s excelled as bombers. Fears of structural weakness proved groundless; the Republic plane could absorb major battle damage and still return home. A major leap in performance came in 1950, with the introduction of the swept wing F-84F Thunderstreak, virtually a new airplane when compared with its straight-wing predecessor.

1950-1959

Visions of planes
in every garage are put aside
even as Cold War tensions
bring war in Korea.
Airline travel flourishes again
as the piston engine
reaches its apogee, then
withers, forced aside
by exciting new
ocean spanning jets.

1950
Lockheed L-1049 Constellation

Lockheed's triple-tailed beauty, the Constellation, was supremely efficient and speedy, and also extremely photogenic. She and her competitors, the Douglas DC-6 and the Boeing Stratocruiser, put the world's airlines back on the path of interconnecting the globe halted by World War II. In 1939, Howard Hughes, owner of Transcontinental and Western Air (TWA), and an experienced aircraft designer, worked with Lockheed to develop a long-ranged "aircraft of the future." Hughes being a perfectionist,

the L-1049 Constellation made no compromises in streamlining. The complex curvature of its airfoil-shaped fuselage was a nightmare to manufacture.

But the plane performed wonderfully; even though the first twenty "Connies" were commandeered by Army Transport Command, by the end of the war, the plane—with its B-29 type engines and 350 mph top speed—was still state of the art. Lockheed put the Constellation back into production immediately. By 1946, Pan Am and TWA had started coast-to-coast and trans-Atlantic service. In May of 1950, to reflect its world-spanning abilities, TWA became Trans World Airlines.

This beautifully restored Constellation, baking in the sun outside of Tucson, Arizona, sports TWA's striking twin bands of red on fuselage and tail.

1951
Martin 4-0-4

The Glen Martin Company's last civil aircraft had been the giant China Clipper flying boat of the thirties, but in 1946 the company flew its entrant in the "DC-3 replacement" sweepstakes, the Martin 2-0-2. Beating rival Convair into airline service by six-and-one-half months, the Martin plane looked like a real winner. Bearing some resemblance to the wartime B-26 and sporting the same powerful Pratt and Whitney engines, the 2-0-2 carried forty passengers and seemed more a replacement for the big, four-engined Douglas DC-4.

But the crash of a 2-0-2 during a storm in 1948 was traced to major structural weakness, and a series of setbacks began for the Martin Company. Glen Martin, the company's founder, was forced out—a victim of harsh re-organization terms—just as the new, larger, pressurized model 4-0-4 signalled a modest turnaround. In October 1951, the first of forty Eastern Air Lines 4-0-4s entered service. They were marked like the one shown here.

1952
Vought F-4U Corsair

Anyone who's heard a Corsair scream past knows why the Japanese called them "Whistling Death." Their eerie sound (from the wing-mounted air scoops) seems to trail a ghostly plane-length behind them. Known as the "bent-wing bird" to American GIs, the Vought F-4U Corsair received its peculiar inverted gull wings to keep its landing gear from being too stalky while allowing clearance for a huge, four-blade prop. The 2,000 hp turning this prop was almost too much to handle—the Corsair, in service on land from 1942, wasn't permitted to fly from carriers until December 1944. By August 1945, Navy and Marine F-4U pilots had downed 2,660 enemy planes.

After the war, those writing off the Corsair as obsolete were proved dead wrong with the start of the Korean "Police Action." F-4Us could carry bombs, napalm, and rockets, and so were valuable in the close support and ground attack role. In fact, the production line stayed open till the end of 1952, building Vought AU-1s, which were specially adapted ground-attack Corsairs. Radar-equipped night fighter versions had some success as well. Corsairs saw action in the Suez with the French; some served long years in Latin American Air Forces. Today, their long-nosed good looks make them a favorite with warbird fans.

1953
North American F-86 Sabre

The North American F-86 Sabre captured the popular fancy just as her forebear the Mustang had. A good case can be made that an entire generation of cars from the fifties were inspired by the Sabrejet's looks. Compared to its natural enemy over Korea, the MiG-15, the Sabre was certainly a more elegant design and could crack Mach 1 in a dive. But the MiG was no pushover. Lighter, smaller, and faster at higher altitudes than the F-86, well-trained Russian or Chinese pilots would always hold the initial advantage. And Air Force Sabres usually were at the limits of their range when fighting began over North Korea's MiG Alley, even with drop tanks.

By 1953, with the advent of the F-86F to oppose the MiG-15bis, both fighters were on equal footing and the better training and gunnery of the Americans proved the deciding factor. As the Korean cease-fire took effect, the fighter vs. fighter kill ratio stood at 7 to 1, advantage Sabre.

U.S. AIR FORCE F-86A-7-NA
A.F. SERIAL NO. 48-178

1954
Fairchild C-119 Boxcar

On May 5, 1954, "Earthquake McGoon" flew his mortally damaged C-119 into the side of a hill near Dien Bien Phu, Indochina. "McGoon," real name James McGovern, was a mercenary, flying C-119s clandestinely lent by the U.S. Air Force to Civil Air Transport, heirs to the legendary Flying Tigers of early World War II fame, and soon to be the CIA's proxy air carrier. CAT was flying relief and med evac missions into Dien Bien Phu in a desperate, last-ditch effort to supply French troops surrounded by Viet Minh forces. Two days later, French forces surrendered in place after suffering horrendous losses. Thus, with this odd unwarlike cargo plane began U.S. involvement in Vietnam.

Fairchild began production of this successor to the World War II era C-82 Packet in 1949. The C-119 Boxcar's curious twin-boom layout was optimal for quick on-and-off loading of troops and cargo; in addition, the clam-shell loading doors could be removed for paradropping. In 1968, after serving for many years in Korea and around the world, the Boxcar mutated into a combat plane, the AC-119 Shadow or Stinger gunship, and went back to Vietnam for blood. Packed with six-barrel miniguns and cannon, the gunships would fly steep banked turns in darkness, raining fire down upon the center of a deadly circle.

A more peaceable C-119 is shown here, preserved by the Mid Atlantic Air Museum in Pennsylvania.

1955
Saab J-35 Draken

The "double-delta" wing used in Saab's Mach 2 J-35 Draken interceptor has never been used in its pure form in any other aircraft. Neutral Sweden has always gone it alone in its defense industry; the Draken's descendants, the J-37 Viggen and the new JAS-39 Gripen are also unique designs.

When the Saab J-35 first flew on October 25, 1955, it was perceived as a counter to high-flying Soviet jet bombers. Hence the need for speed and climb. Later marks of the Draken could climb 50,000 feet in one minute. Take off and landing were critical as well, since portions of Swedish highways are used as tactical air strips. The large-area, double-delta wing proved perfect for this, and also provided plenty of room for fuel and equipment.

The J-35 shown here is held by the French Air Museum in Paris, wearing its original camoflage colors. Roundel markings consist of three crowns in Swedish Royal colors of blue and yellow. Drakens flew also with Finland, Denmark, and Austria, but virtually all of the more than 600 built are now retired.

1956
Grumman TBM Avenger

As the Suez crisis heated up into a shooting war in the fall of 1956, Great Britain and France found themselves forced to call upon a motley selection of warplanes. Among the oldest used by both navies was a World War II era American carrier plane, the Grumman TBM/TBF Avenger. The Avenger had flown in 1941, the big torpedo bomber proving its worth as early as the Battle of Midway. But the poor

reliability of its internally carried torpedo nearly sabotaged the TBM early in the war.

As they aged, TBMs grew a profusion of tumor-like domes and pods, and took up anti-submarine and early warning roles. It was as early warning aircraft that the Avengers took part in their last shooting war, serving with HMS *Bulwark* of the Royal Navy in

support of the Suez invasion. The French Aeronavale also daubed a few with the yellow and black invasion stripes. None, so far as is known, came under enemy fire.

A fuselage big enough to carry a 22-inch diameter torpedo internally made for a superb water bomber to fight forest fires after the war.

1957
Lockheed L-188 Electra

When the Lockheed L-188 Electra first flew on December 6, 1957, it seemed to have a secure future. Reviving the name of Lockheed's elegant, first all-metal transport from the thirties, the four-turboprop plane had been designed partly as a response to the earlier Vickers Viscount prop-jet, and partly to meet an American Airlines requirement for an eighty- to one-hundred-seat, intermediate-range airliner. Fuel guzzling jets were still felt to be uneconomical for shorter routes and the Electra, as the only large American turboprop, picked up many orders.

Unfortunately, two suspicious crashes just after entry into airline service were traced to structural failures. This led, in 1960, to year-long speed restrictions that hampered operations until a brawnier model, the Electra II, was introduced. The highly publicized crashes, coupled with the airlines' rush to buy new jets, put a damper on all but token further sales of the plane. Luckily for Lockheed, work had already begun on what became the successful Electra-based P-3 Orion series of naval reconnaissance planes. These are still in production.

KLM was the only European user of the Electra. This one is seen at Amsterdam's Schilpol airport in the mid-sixties.

1958
Grumman F-11F Tiger

A very petite Tiger! But the F-11F proved to be an unlucky design, even though its slim, "Coke bottle" fuselage and thin wings made it the first supersonic Navy fighter. These very features kept the Tiger short ranged and unable to carry much of a warload, and when the F-8U Crusader came along, the Tiger seemed more like a pussycat. Even in early testing, the Tiger was jinxed; when firing its four 20mm cannon in a Mach 1 dive, the prototype-11F crossed the path of the spent shells and shot itself down! An uprated Tiger F-11F-1F with a new engine set a world altitude record of 76,932 feet on April 18, 1958, which, typically for the luckless Tiger , stood for all of two weeks.

However, the Tiger looked tailor-made for the Blue Angels, the Navy aerobatic team. Fast, agile, and with a noisy afterburner to thrill the crowds, the F-11F flew in the Angels' blue and gold for more than ten years. Perhaps the most compelling reason

for keeping the Tiger so long was— the navy no longer needed them elsewhere.

The USS Intrepid Museum in New York City keeps a Tiger on display in the lightning bolt markings of VF-33 fighter squadron, "The Astronauts," as flown from her decks in 1958.

1959
Douglas DC-4 and DC-7

The DC-4 and its clones, the DC-6 and DC-7, were the peak of prop liner evolution. Sturdier, easier to build, and with tamer engines, they had the edge over the Lockheed Constellation.

Developed as a wartime stretch of the four-engined DC-4 whose civilian career had been cut short, the DC-6 was seen as a military transport, but with peace came tremendous interest by the airlines. By 1947, United Air

Lines Mainliners cruising in the stratosphere at 300+ mph could cross the country in ten hours with only one stop. American Airlines, just as it had with the DC-3, urged construction of even larger, faster versions to beat the Super Connies of TWA. Thus the DC-7 and her seven-seas spanning sister, the DC-7C, came about.

But the shadow of the swept-wing Boeing 707 hung over the later years of the Douglas piston transports. The 707 had flown as early as 1954, and a contract with Pan American soon followed. By October 1959, transatlantic

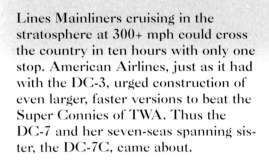

1958-1959

service began with Pan Am's 707 Clippers. Quickly, DC-7s were phased out, just as the last DC-7C's were delivered to KLM.

The big "Dougs" drifted down the food chain of aviation, eventually hauling freight and contraband. Today, they still litter airfields like Miami and Recife—tramp steamers of the air.

1960
Fouga C.M. 170 Magister

The petite, butterfly-tailed Fouga Magister would seem hardly fit for use in a shooting war. Yet she has seen more combat than many battle-scarred veteran fighter planes in this book. In 1960, Moise Tshombe led Katanga province in its secession from the former Belgian Congo. He realized the value of air power, jet airpower especially, and purchased two of the inexpensive trainers, along with a motley collection of prop planes. Fitted with bomb racks and two forward-firing machine guns, the Magisters, piloted by a shadowy bunch of mercenaries, helped hold off a force of United Nations peace keepers 10,000 strong.

Originally flown in 1952, the French "Fouga" was the first true jet basic trainer. Developed from a line of Fouga jet sailplanes, whose long wings she inherits, the 400 mph Magister was made possible by the advent of

tiny, low-powered jet engines from the Turbomeca firm; 916 were built.

Magisters saw action with Israel in the 1967 Six Day War, and battled Polisario guerrillas in the former Spanish Sahara. Many air forces used the plane more peacefully in their brightly colored aerobatic teams, and increasing numbers are appearing in private hands, as shown here at the annual Valiant Air Command meet in Titusville, Florida.

1960-1969

Brush fire wars and a major conflagration called Vietnam bring together all manner of odd warplanes. Airpower seems unable to prevail in this quagmire. As the war divides the country, some sporting machines provide much needed light relief.

1961
Piasecki H-21
Shawnee

Forever tagged "Flying Banana" by the press, the H-21 was called the "Shawnee" by the U.S. Army and the "Workhorse" by the Piasecki company. By 1961, the twin-rotored helicopter was reaching the end of its service life because it lacked one of the new turbine engines. But its very age

and the ability to carry 16 troops meant the H-21 could be risked in one of the opening gambits of what would become the Vietnam War.

The South Vietnamese Army always seemed to need more and more "advisors" and air support from the United States. As a result, on December 2, 1961, two Shawnee-equipped U.S. Army companies arrived from Fort Bragg and Fort Lewis. Before the end of the year, they had flown their first support missions and began to draw heavy ground fire from the Viet Cong. Hurriedly, thirty caliber machine guns were welded to stanchions in the cargo doors.

In 1962, three more helicopter companies were deployed. By 1969, the Shawnee had retired from the field, but the Army's First Aviation Brigade alone had nearly 3,600 helicopters in Vietnam. Shawnees such as this U.S. Air Force survivor seen resting in the dust of the March Field Museum in Riverside, California, wrote the first pages of the combat manual for what would be called the "Helicopter War."

300

RESCUE

JET INTAKE DANGER

BEWARE

1962
Douglas A-4
Skyhawk

In 1953, Ed Heineman had a problem: he had complained to government officials about the escalating weight and complexity of military planes. As design head of Douglas aircraft, he was expected to come up with a new attack plane that would reverse these trends. His solution, the Douglas A-4D Skyhawk, known as "Heineman's Hot Rod," flew in August 1954. The new delta-winged jet could carry nuclear and other weapons equal to its own empty weight and grossed out at half the projected 30,000 pounds. It was definitely small, its wingspan less than the World War I Sopwith Camel, so no wing folding would be needed on carrier decks. It was fast—700 mph, and cheap—less than one-million dollars each. The navy and the marines ordered hundreds.

By December 1962, a much-improved Skyhawk flew with the new J-52 engine, allowing two-seat trainer versions and upgraded avionics. When production finally ended in 1979, about 3,000 had been built. The A-4 served aboard the USS Intrepid and a preserved example on her museum flight deck looks ready for flight even today. After tours in Vietnam, the Skyhawk found a new calling as a dogfighter for "Top Gun" and other aggressor squadrons. Some will probably be flying with Reserve units until 2005 and for other nations long after that.

1963
Boeing C-97 Stratotanker

In 1963, when the Illinois Air National Guard began equipping its KC-97 Stratotankers with under-wing jet pods, the lifespan of the aging "flying fuel tank" was extended by fifteen more years. The in-flight refueling KC-97 appears in these photos.

Yet the B-29 derived design had a more glamorous cousin: the deluxe, ocean-spanning, double-decker Stratocruiser. In the early fifties, both Pan Am and Northwest had them, but this airliner really was the last gasp of pre-World War II Imperial Airways, the parent of BOAC. British Overseas Air's "Monarch" London–New York service provided "impeccable service...food an epicure's delight...luxurious lower deck lounge with well stocked bar." Early James Bond novels are filled with nostalgic details of these flights.

The brochures didn't mention the planes' temperamental 28-cylinder engines, however, which led to a lot of three-engine flying, nor the Boeing's marginal range, which forced many "non-stop" trans-atlantic flights to use Newfoundland, Iceland, or Ireland as refueling stops. People might wax nostalgic about the old Stratocruisers, but they rushed to board the new jets.

110

1964
Lockheed SR-71 Blackbird

When President LyndonJohnson revealed the SR-71 to the American public on television in July 1964, most viewers just blinked, looked surprised, and then turned to the sports news. The ten years just past had seen new aeronautical miracles almost daily. A Mach 3 spyplane that cruised at 80,000 feet was only par for the course. It is only with thirty-five years hindsight that we fully appreciate the advance the Blackbird represented then, and, in some senses, still represents today.

Designer Kelly Johnson and the Lockheed Skunk Works had invented whole industries from scratch. They worked voodoo with titanium, a much stronger and more heat-resistant metal

than aluminum, but one which disintegrated if touched by cadmium-plated wrenches or felt-tipped pens. They built titanium wings, corrugated to stop heat deformation, which seeped fuel, a strange non-flammable fuel called "Lockheed lighter fluid #2." They devised aluminum impregnated tires to reflect heat. Most importantly, they designed radar-reducing paint, and the first "stealthy" design features of any plane. This last feature, and an ability to cruise for hours at 2200 mph explains why no SR-71 was ever shot down or intercepted, though many tried. When the Blackbirds were retired right before the Gulf War, the loss was keenly felt. A few have been brought back, but most are now in museums, such as these in Mobile, Alabama, and March Field,California.

1965
Douglas AD
Skyraider

In 1965, as the conflict in Vietnam widened and became simply "the War," the Skyraider was there. The venerable attack bomber had been there from the beginning in 1960, when only prop planes were allowed by the 1954 Geneva treaty, and she would be there at the end in 1974, as the South Vietnamese took them out of mothballs to fly their last hopeless missions.

Designed literally on the back of an envelope in 1944 by the prolific Ed Heineman, the Douglas heavy lifter just missed action in World War II, but proved its worth in Korea. In Vietnam, the big jets just could not match the "Able Dog's" ability to loiter over a battle field. First used by the South Vietnamese with American "advisors," then by the U.S. Navy and

Marines, finally even the air force took some on charge. Most of the kids working on the Douglas Skyraiders thought she looked old; World War I old. So they called her the SPAD, though some said it stood for Single Place, Attack, Douglas. Later, she was Sandy, for Search AND Destroy missions flown with rescue helicopters.

A pristine A-1 in USS Intrepid squadron VA-176 "Bumblebee" markings is pictured. A Spad from another squadron off the USS Midway actually shot down a MiG-17 in June 1965.

1966 Lockheed C-130 Hercules

Great Britain had been slow to recognize the sterling qualities of the Lockheed C-130. Not until October 1966 did the first C-130K model fly for the RAF. First flown twelve years earlier, they shouldered every job the military could throw at them. Even now, fifty years later, a new model Hercules is in development: the scimitar prop-bladed C-130J. The Herk combined turboprop engines and a drop-down, drive-in, low-mounted cargo hold with short take-off and landing from unprepared fields. Although larger planes such as the C-5 must carry oversize items, and the new four-jet C-17 can get there faster, the C-130's all-round abilities have never been beaten.

Much like the C-47 Dakotas that flew over every World War II battle-

field, the Hercules has been the work-horse of many air forces all through the second half of this century. They've been used in more bellicose ways as well, bristling with side-mounted cannons as gun ships and dropping 15,000-pound fuel-air bombs in the Gulf War.

Later C-130s don't really need JATO rockets for short takeoff performance, but it does get your attention at an air-show!

1967-1968

A fighter without a gun! When the F-4 Phantom began flying combat air patrols over Vietnam in 1964, U.S. pilots believed their hot new fighter could handle any threat with short-range Sidewinders or new long-range radar-guided Sparrow missiles. They were horribly mistaken. The Sparrows were untrustworthy and limited by crippling "Rules of Engagement." The agile North Vietnamese MiG-17's and speedy MiG-21's could avoid the F-4s

which, most un-Phantom like, were visible for miles due to smoky engines and their hulking size.

In 1966, U.S. Air Force Phantoms were fitted with a gunpod containing a Vulcan rotary barreled "Gatling Gun" cannon. By 1967, the combination of gun armament and new tactics by air force aces such as Robin Olds began to turn the tide. The navy disdained the cannon armament, concentrating

on improving missile reliability and flying technique. From this evolved the Top Gun dog fighting school. Although a landmark warplane by all standards, with 5,000 built, the 1991 Gulf War was the Phantom's swan song in U.S. military service. In its last battles, the F-4G Wild Weasel dug out and ripped up enemy radar with a suite of advanced electronic counter measures and HARM missiles that rode down radar beams to their source.

1968 Boeing B-52 Stratofortress

As powerful a symbol as it was a weapon, in 1968 the jagged shape of the B-52 came to represent for anti-war activists all that was wrong with American policy in Vietnam. Flags and posters showed B-52s dropping their loads over screaming children and fields of flowers. But from 1965 on, the U.S. military had considered the B-52 to be the only sure way of forcing the Viet Cong and the North Vietnamese government to negotiate.

When the B-52 began flying in 1952, it was seen only as a means to deliver thermonuclear destruction to the Soviet heartland. Boeing scaled up their earlier six-jet B-47 into the 185-foot span Stratofortress. More than 500 were built; in the process Boeing found they had made a plane with an endless capacity to adapt to new roles and an almost infinite fatigue life. As Soviet defenses improved, B-52s acquired stand-off missiles and decoys. Over Vietnam, up to 45 tons of bombs were hung on what was now called the BUFF or Big Ugly Fat Fella. Iron bombs were still the weapon of choice in the Gulf War, along with fancy new cruise missiles. By the time the BUFF retires in 2035 or so, most of the men who first flew her will be retired or dead. Five generations of electronics will have been installed and ripped out. New engines are not out of the question either, as the eight TF-33 jets may be replaced with four much more powerful Rolls-Royce RB.211s on today's remaining ninety-plus B-52H models.

1969
Grumman F-8F
Bearcat

Almost twenty-five years to the day after its first flight, the Grumman F8F Bearcat fighter finally came into its own. On August 16, 1969, battling only against the clock in the quiet skies over the Mojave, a Bearcat flown by Lockheed test pilot Darryl Greenamyer broke a world's speed record for prop-driven aircraft that had stood for thirty years. He averaged 483 mph over the 3 km course, besting the mark set by a German Messerschmitt Bf-109R right before World War II began.

Though ousted from front-line service by more promising jet fighters, such as the Banshee and the Panther, the tiny Grumman fighter had found its niche when civilian unlimited air racing was revived at Reno, Nevada, in 1964. Indeed,Greenamyer and his plane, named Conquest I, had dominated Reno for five years as a pylon racer. Conquest I was greatly modified from the one shown in these photos, with a tiny bubble canopy, seven feet clipped from the wings, and a 3300+ hp engine. The Bearcat would hold the record for ten more years.

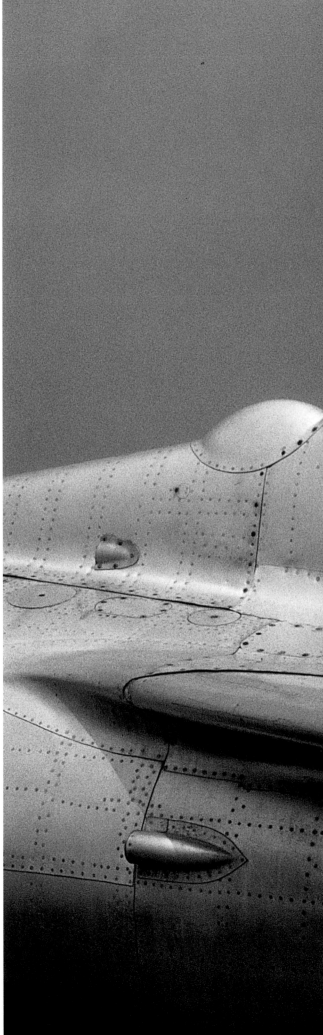

1970
Pitts S-1/S-2 Special

As record-setting airplanes go, there could not be more difference between the Pitts Special and the Bearcat. The tiny Pitts might look like something from the twenties—and it does have a long history, first flying in 1945 or so—but they remain competitive in racing and aerobatics even today. Aerobatic pilot Betty Skelton was the first to order a Pitts Special for display in 1947 and although later models sport 200 hp engines, the basic qualities are unchanged: precise control, great structural strength, and power to burn.

Certainly a high point for the Pitts came in the summer of 1970 at the World Aerobatic Championship held in Hullington England, when the American men's team of Bob Henredeen, Charlie Hillard and Gene Soucy—each flying a bright red Pitts Special—won the Nesterov Cup, the team trophy, for the first time. Lately, however, Russian Yaks and Sukhois have stolen some thunder from the little Pitts. Yet at an airshow, nothing beats a Pitts snarling straight up in a seemingly endless series of rolls or formation flying with less than ten feet between wingtips at 200 mph.

1970-1979

America begins an agonizing withdrawl from Vietnam with support from a few magnificent Navy airplanes. Some old campaigners, both military and civilian, have another moment of fame on very different battlefields as this unsettled decade ends.

1971
Vought A-7
Corsair II

The first A-7 wing of the U.S. Air Force reached full readiness by July 1971, marking the adoption by the air force of yet another navy combat plane, much as they had with the F-4 Phantom II.

In 1965, Vought designers took the basic layout of the "Gunfighter" F-8U Crusader, chopped the speed, hung up to 15,000 pounds of ordnance under its wings, and added a revolutionary navigation and aiming system. The navy's A-7, though under-powered at first, grew to be a worthy successor to the A-4 Skyhawk.

When the air force saw how perfectly fitted to Vietnam operations the plane was, they requested their own. The land-based A-7D was used as a low-level tactical fighter and, amazingly, as replacement for the old prop-driven A-1 Sandy. When daubed with air force drab camouflage, the Corsair became the SLUF or Short Little Ugly Fella.

The A-7's pinpoint accuracy and long range kept it a valuable asset into the nineties, though after the Gulf War it was phased out of first-line U.S. military service. The photos shown here are Naval Reserve Corsair Es from CVWR-20 on the USS *"Eisenhower"* in 1989.

1972
Mikoyan Gurevich   MiG-17F "Fresco"

A late fifties update of the MiG-15, the larger, more capable MiG-17 "Fresco" reached the apex of its combat career in 1972. On May 10, in an epic dogfight, a North Vietnamese MiG fought the U.S. Navy's newest fighter to a standstill. A McDonnell F-4J "Phantom" piloted by then Lt. Randy Cunningham finally spiked the MiG with a Sidewinder missile only after pitting everything he had learned in the new "Top Gun" air combat program against the brilliantly flown plane.

Fliers still argue whether the legendary Vietnamese ace Pham Tuan—nicknamed "Colonel Toon" by the Russians—piloted the MiG on that day. Cunningham still believes this, but Tuan is still alive, and, so far, silent on the subject. Another NVNAF ace, Col. Nguyen Van Coc, who died that day, was most probably the pilot.

The San Diego Museum's "Fresco F," shown with Lt. Cunningham's Phantom number "100" in pursuit, actually served with the East German, and later the Egyptian Air Force. Its garish paint scheme is close to that of a NVNAF ace's plane shown to Japanese photographers not long before the fateful dogfight.

1973
Grumman A-6 Intruder

After January 1973, all American aircraft withdrew from Vietnam; the last task remaining was clearing mines dropped into Haiphong Harbor by Grumman Intruders and other U.S. Navy bombers.

When Grumman produced the twin-engined, all-weather attack bomber in the early sixties, it seemed more a relic of the fifties, with mildly swept wings, wide dumpy fuselage, and underslung engines. A subsonic plane! Inside, however, was DIANE, a magical new computerized navigational and bombing system. When DIANE behaved, the formidable weather over Hanoi became an ally, hiding attacking Intruders on their trips "downtown."

The Intruder shown here sports the tail markings of VA-85 Squadron, at that time called the Black Falcons, the

second unit to take the A-6 into battle in 1965. It carries a refueling hose pod between its engines.

The Intruder was one of the first navy aircraft to deploy to the Persian Gulf in 1991. It performed well, but the navy has retired all the bomber types, leaving only the Electronic Warfare EA6-B Prowlers. These heavier four-man Intruder derivatives are taking over the duties of air force craft like the F-4G Wild Weasel and EF-111 Ravens.

1974 Boeing 727

In January 1974, Delta Airlines took delivery of the 1,000th Boeing 727, making the Seattle tri-jet first in the world to reach that mark. When production ended in 1984, more than 1,800 had been sold and more than half that number are still flying today.

Key to the 727's success as a short-to-medium haul jet was its advanced wing design. Most everyone who's flown on one has noticed how the wing seems, alarmingly, to "disassemble" itself for landing, with leading edge slats and rear-mounted, triple-slotted, Fowler-type flaps rolling out on their screw jacks. When the upper wing-mounted spoilers pop up you can see right through the wing! These high-lift devices were essential for getting in and out of 5,000-foot-long airfields in the smaller cities that were now being opened up to jets. The 727's commonality with its big brother, the 707, in passenger cabin width and cockpit layout helped sell the airlines as well, even in the "stagflation" years of the late seventies. Although entry into service in the mid-sixties was marred by crashes caused by "deep stalling" of the 727's high T-tail, the plane went on to become a totally reliable workhorse.

Grumman E-2

A plane with its own umbrella, the huge, twenty-four foot rotating Frisbee on top of Grumman's E-2 is a radar antenna devoted to airborne early warning (AEW) for the Fleet. The E-2s are first off the flat-tops and last to land, so vital are their duties as "flying control tower" during carrier maneuvers. Incidentally, those huge radomes make them a bear to land.

The first E-2s entered service in 1964, just in time for carrier operations in the Vietnam War. They were designed as replacements for the little WF-1 "Willy Fudd" AEW planes from the fifties. An anti-sub version of that earlier plane, known as the S-2F Trader, or by its crews as the "Stoof," had no radome and is shown below. The latest variant of the Hawkeye, the E-2C, was completing its acceptance trials aboard the USS Saratoga in early 1975. Now, advanced versions called Group II and Hawkeye 2000 will be created by retrofitting existing E-2s and by building some new aircraft in 2000—forty years after the Hawkeye's maiden flight. These new planes can scan six million cubic miles of airspace while tracking more than 2,000 targets at once.

1976
Grumman HU-16 Albatross

On August 13, 1976, the U.S. Navy gave up its last flying boat, a Grumman Albatross, delivered to the Navy Air Museum at Pensacola, Florida. Since 1911, the navy had used seaplanes, flying boats, and amphibians for bombing, scouting, and patrol craft. Now carrier-borne craft and helicopters handled these duties. Only Russia and Japan continue to build new military flying boats.

The Albatross had first flown in 1947, as a larger successor to the Grumman Goose and Mallard amphibians. Aside from its flying boat hull, the Albatross has retractable wheels for use on land. Although first envisioned as anti-submarine planes for the navy, both the navy and air force used them for utility duties, most importantly, sea-air rescue. In Korea and Vietnam, hundreds of downed airmen were scooped from the sea. Gradually, however, helicopters took over this role. A few Albatross soldier on for other nations, and a few fly commercially, but as with this example, most survivors reside in museums.

The unmistakable butterfly tail of the Beech Bonanza.—what better sign of Victory was there for the post World War II civil flying world than the sporty V-tail of the Bonanza, among the most advanced of all the smart new ships offered to a plane-hungry public. Even before production began in 1947, Beechcraft had 1,500 on back order. Continuing Walter Beech's tradition of design innovation shown in the Model 17 Staggerwing and the

Model 18 Twin Beech, the Bonanza offered tricycle landing gear, 200 mph speed, and limousine-like comfort for four in its futuristic, curved Plexiglas-enclosed cabin.

In 1977, exactly thirty years after the first was delivered, Bonanza number ten-thousand came off the line. The V-tail had long since been given up for a conventional swept fin and horizontal tail as an ever more cautious and

litigous public convinced Beech that the Bonanza's trademark tail was too tricky. Over the next twenty years, minor airframe refinements were made; engine and avionics were kept state of the art. Now at the turn of the millenium, incredibly, the Bonanza is still being built. The century's longest aircraft production run continues with no end in sight.

1978
Hawker Sea Fury FB.11

A World War II vintage airplane wins pride of place for the year 1978. On September 17th, a Hawker Sea Fury named "Baby Gorilla" and flown by Lloyd Hamilton broke a five-year Bearcat and Mustang monopoly by qualifying for the unlimited Gold Race at Reno, Nevada. Though he finished only sixth, Sea Furies have been strong competitors at Reno ever since.

The Sea Fury traces its pedigree from the Battle of Britain Hurricane and the thirties-era Fury for which she is named. First flight was in 1944. That five-bladed prop was about the limit for wartime technology, and it is spun by a 3400 hp Bristol Centaurus engine which gave speeds of 460 mph. More than five-hundred Sea Furys served in the Royal Navy during the Korean Conflict. They were used to great effect as bombers, and at least one MiG-15 fell to its guns.

Hamilton's ex-Australian Navy Sea Fury is pictured here wearing the same Aussie camoflage and markings she wore at Reno in 1978. The plane is almost completely "stock," without the speed modifications that disfigure many other racing Furys. The indomitable Sea Fury will very likely be racing well into the twenty-first century, assuming such races are still permitted. At least one has raced successfully with a huge 28-cylinder "corncob" engine like those used on the giant B-36 bomber.

1979
Mikoyan Gurevich MiG-21

June 27, 1979, was not a good day for the MiG-21 Fishbed. In the dangerous skies over southern Lebanon that day, six of Israel's new F-15 fighters won their first kills by luring a like number of Syrian MiGs to their destruction.

The MiGs were overmatched, but in 1958, when the silver, Mach 2, delta-winged interceptors first entered Soviet service, few planes in the west could top them. Small, agile, easy to fly and maintain, if a bit rough in surface finish—as our photos show—they were also cheap. The Soviets poured them out to Warsaw Pact nations and client states; from Vietnam to Cuba, eleven thousand went to more than thirty countries. They have fought in more conflicts than possibly any other combat plane, increasingly on the losing side, until by the early eighties they were totally outclassed.

Ironically, the MiG-21 will be kept flying into the 21st century partly through Israeli efforts. Electronics firms there are marketing a suite of modernization kits for older Fishbeds that brings their cockpit, avionics, and armament to state-of-the-art standards.

133

1980
Dornier Do-228

Representing a new wing shape from an old company, the Dornier Do-228 commuter airliner was constructed in 1980, and first flew on March 28, 1981. Its eye-catching, high-lift wing continued the company's legacy of innovation in such aircraft as the 1929 giant, twelve-engined DO-X flying boat and the World War II Do-17 "Flying Pencil" bomber. The wing, originally dubbed TNT for "new technology," with its distinctive, low-drag triangular tips, supercritical section and composite construction, was fitted to a stretched fuselage developed from the smaller DO-28 Skyservant in 1979. With wing-mounted, twin 700 hp turboprops and a new tricycle gear, the result has been a commercial success for Dornier, with around 250 sold.

The short takeoff and landing (STOL) DO-228 can carry fifteen to nineteen passengers. Its scimitar wing has appeared over Antarctica, Nigeria, Mali, and many other countries, including the United States. This one was caught over Hartford, Connecticut.

The DO-328, a newer thirty- to forty-seat version with the same wing but a totally new fuselage, has also sold well.

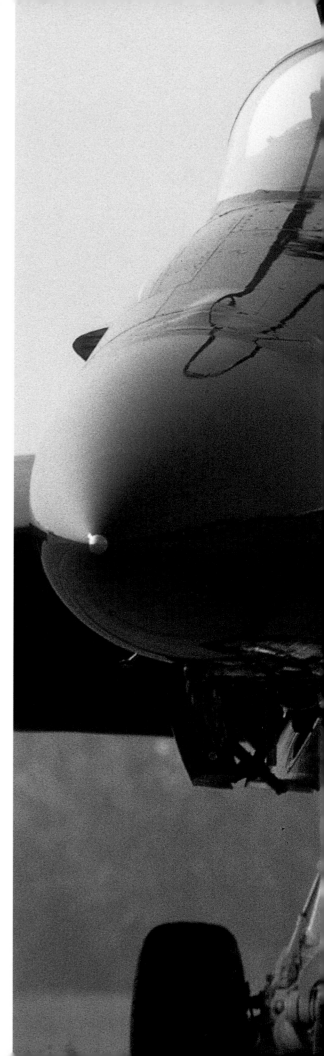

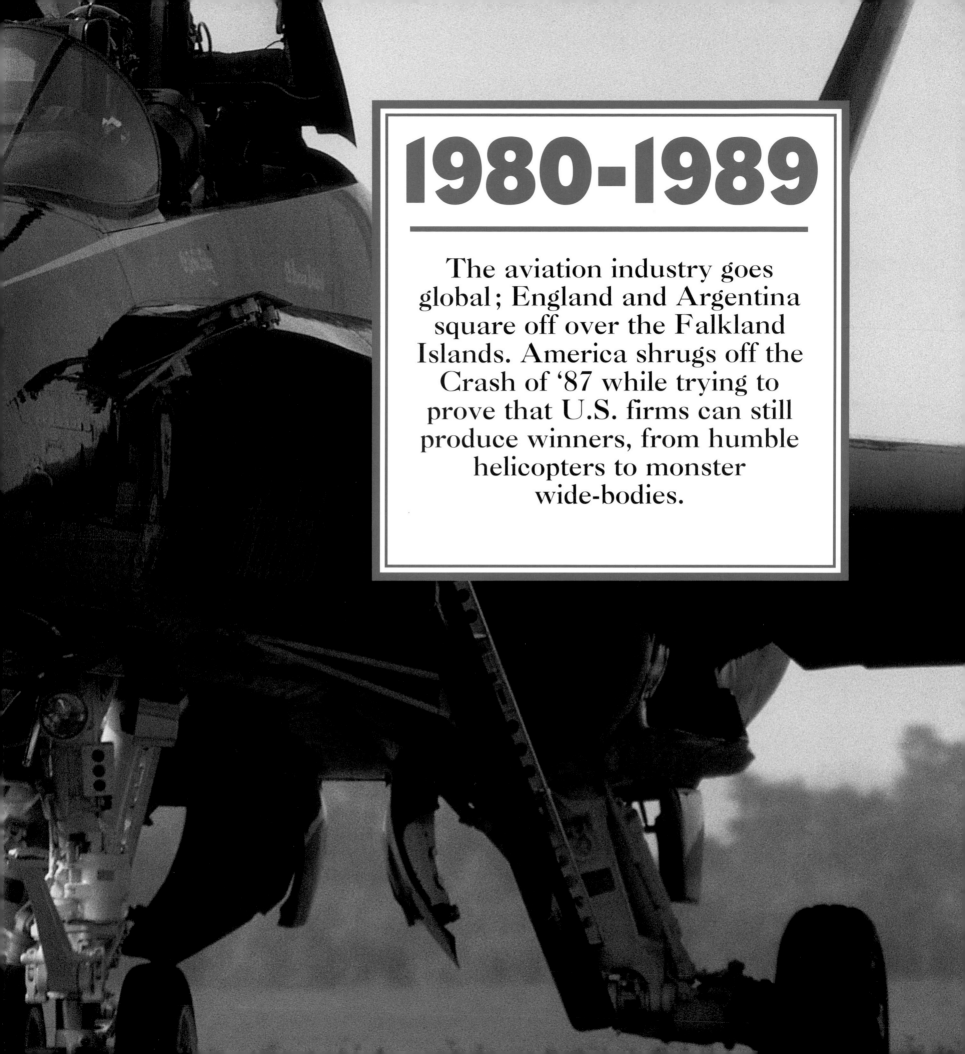

1980-1989

The aviation industry goes global; England and Argentina square off over the Falkland Islands. America shrugs off the Crash of '87 while trying to prove that U.S. firms can still produce winners, from humble helicopters to monster wide-bodies.

1981
Let Z-37A Cmelak
(Bumblebee)

With the built-from-mismatched-spare-parts look that most agricultural planes have, the Czechoslovak Cmelak, or Bumblebee is no beauty. Like her namesake though, the Z-37 is maneuverable and agile, qualities needed to get into the small farm plots

of Eastern Europe and deliver accurately up to a ton of chemicals.

Though Poland was ostensibly the Ag plane center for the Warsaw Pact countries, the Czech firm Let produced a competent design in 1963, and by the late seventies it had sold about 700 examples to countries as

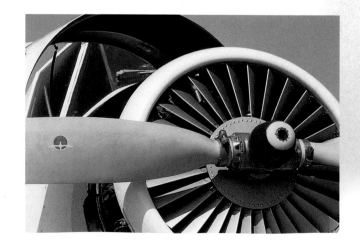

diverse as India, Iraq, and the United Kingdom. In 1981, a turboprop-powered version flew and the Z-37T, built now by Zlin, became the new production standard. There is even a two-place trainer version available.

These views of an American-owned Z-37 show off the plane's superb visibility from its high-mounted cabin, a must when skimming only fifteen feet above the crops.

1982
British Aerospace Harrier

Since its first flight in 1960, the Harrier VTOL fighter has had to struggle to be taken seriously as a warplane. In May 1982, it gained the respect it had sought for twenty-two years, when the British began the battle to retake the Falkland Islands from Argentina. British Navy Sea Harriers, catapulting from odd "ski jump" carriers, won air superiority over Argentine fighters and bombers. The first kill was a Dassault Mirage downed by a Sidewinder missile fired from an 801 Squadron Sea Harrier on May 1st. In addition, RAF Harriers flew ground attack against occupying forces as British infantry finally took the capital of Port Stanley on June 14th.

The first operational Harriers built in 1969 had limited payload capabilities, but gradual improvements in their Pegasus lift engines led to interest by the U.S. Marine Corps in the Harrier's ability to fly close air support missions from unprepared fields. The photos show the Mc Donnell Douglas-built AV-8B, one of the latest Marine Harriers, demonstrating its unique hovering abilities. The marines battle-tested their Harriers in the Gulf War.

1983
Westland/Sikorsky Sea King

Battlefield companion to the Harrier in the Falklands War was the Westland Sea King helicopter, used as a workhorse during troop landings. Unfortunately, an airborne early-warning version was too late to provide protection to the fleet during the fighting. By 1983, a run of nine quickly-modified conversions had been put in service.

Westland developed the Sea King directly from the American Sikorsky

copter of the same name, using the engine and rotor layout, and keeping the same "boat fuselage" design that made the Vietnam-era U.S. Air Force rescue version, called the "Jolly Green Giant," so recognizable. Canada used the Sea King, too, as evidenced by our photo of one of their CH-124s. Note the radar "thimble" in back of the rotor.

Sikorsky's original design dates from 1960 and has been used to ferry astronauts and presidents, but it was built for anti-submarine warfare, at which it still excels. Still, forty years is a long time for a helicopter design to last; the U.S. Coast Guard has retired theirs and many more in military use are slated to be replaced by the same company's S-70 Sea Hawk.

1984
Rutan Long-EZ

One of the most prolific and creative designers to appear since the early days of the century, Burt Rutan began flight testing his most famous creation, the world-spanning "Voyager," in June of 1984.

Beginning in 1972 with his first plane for the home-built market, the delta-winged Vari-Viggen, Rutan has used space age materials and innovative aerodynamics to produce a series of unique aircraft. Each uses his trademark canard foreplanes, as illustrated by this photo of the 1981 Long-EZ. So popular are his designs with home builders that every year at the Oshkosh Fly-In of the Experimental Aircraft Association, sixty to a hundred Rutan ships line up in a row called "E-Z Street." His Scaled Composites division has worked on aircraft as diverse as the Beech Starship, the Pond Racer, and a NASA test craft, as well as the Ares low-cost attack plane.

The implausibly slim-winged Voyager, piloted by Burt's brother, Dick Rutan, and Jeanna Yeager, completed its 25,000 mile round-the-world flight nine days after starting out across the Pacific on December 14, 1986. It returned to its starting point at Edwards Air Force Base, California, with fuel for only 500 more miles remaining in its tanks.

141

1985
Mc Donnell Douglas
F/A-18 Hornet

The loser in the 1975 fly-off against the General Dynamics F-16 had, ten years later, emerged a winner. In 1985, while U.S. Navy Hornets were on their first extended shakedown cruise at sea, the first Australian built F-18 flew, helping insure much needed export orders would continue. Today seven other nations also fly the Hornet.

A long, involved design process led from the losing Northrop YF-17 light-weight to the larger, beefier F-18 carrier strike fighter. The U.S. Navy, needing a smaller plane as counterpart to its large F-14 Tomcats, and liking the safety aspects of the twin-engine F-17, asked Mc Donnell Douglas to team up with Northrop to develop a carrier version. At first, the resulting F/A-18 was derided as overweight and short of range. Gradually pilots realized the

Hornet was truly able to handle both air-to-air tasks and strike missions with efficiency; later models have resolved most other problems. Soon the new Super Hornet, a stealthy and, of course, larger development will enter production, eventually replacing almost every combat plane the U.S. Navy now flies.

The Blue Angels aerobatic team began to use the F-18 in 1986, giving up their little A-4 Skyhawks. Although they are early models, the nimble Hornets have added new, high-angle-of-attack routines and look to become the longest serving aircraft of the Blue Angels family.

143

1986
Grumman F-14 Tomcat

Grumman F-14 Tomcats flew top cover as operation El Dorado Canyon began against Libya's Colonel Khadaffi on April 14, 1986. It was not the first time the F-14 had challenged Libya's Air Force and it would not be the last. Tomcats had downed two Libyan Sukhois in 1981, and would later "splash" a pair of MiG-23 Floggers in 1989.

Fleet defense, of course, was the primary mission of the swing-wing Tomcat when it began testing in 1971. Those wings allow slow approach speeds when landing and great "yank-and-bank" maneuverability in a dogfight, while swinging back for high-speed interception far away from the carrier. The proven Phantom formula of two men, two engines was followed and the "guy in back" had lots to do, tracking multiple targets and controlling the superb beyond-visual-range Phoenix missiles.

Engine problems were the Tomcat's one glaring weakness throughout its service life, but at her zenith the Tomcat equipped every carrier in service, thirty-one squadrons in total. Still, over Iraq in 1991, the F-15 seemed to capture the limelight, and the F-14 has begun to yield to the F-18 Hornet and mutate into the "Bombcat" strike aircraft. However, even now, most F-14 pilots would not hesitate to issue the challenge that has been the Tomcat's motto since the beginning: "Anytime, Baby!"

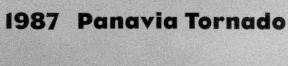

1987 Panavia Tornado

On the first of November, 1987, when the first squadron of British Tornado F.Mk 3 fighters went fully operational, it marked the culmination of long years of testing and production that began in 1968, the year the Panavia consortium of England, Italy, and West Germany was formed to build the MRCA Multi Role Combat Aircraft. The F.Mk 3 is the Air Defense Version of the Tornado and has now become sole heir to the Spitfires and Lightnings that guarded Britain's skies in the past. Other RAF Tornados are charged with low-level strike missions, as happened in the Gulf War. These missions proved to be tough, as flying at "nought feet" over heavily defended Iraqi airfields with pinpoint munitions took its toll. Six planes were lost in the fighting.

Although the Tornado design was advanced, with the swing-wings that were *de rigeur* at the time of its first flight in 1974, the plane's electronics

1987

have kept the plane competitive. With each nation demanding a specialized suite of weapons, from air-launched missiles, to rockets, to runway-cratering bomblets, great flexibility in aiming and targeting had to be built in.

Germany flies about 250 of the 1000 built, most as bombers, such as the one pictured from the Luftwaffe's 38th Geschwader.

1988
Bell UH-1 Huey/Iroquois

So unassuming is the humble "Huey" (never called "Iroquois" by those who flew them) that its role as one of the major combat aircraft of the century is easily forgotten. By 1988, many of the more than thirty nations using them were looking for a replacement. Australia began using the Sikorsky S-70, while the U.S. and others bought the S-60 Black Hawk. The Germans chose to update the UH-1 with new weapons and computers, and the Philippines began taking on refurbished Huey gunships.

Yet 12,000 and more of all models of the Huey were built and—on any given day during its heyday in Vietnam—2,000 could be in the air. From 1962, when the first short-fuselage HU-1s arrived, to the later large-doored versions such as the Army machine in the photo, they took on transport, utility, and medevac or "dustoff" missions. The Huey later morphed into a gunship with multiple protrusions of guns and rocket pods added to protect and escort the unarmed troop-carrying "slicks."

When the new Huey Cobra, a dedicated attack helicopter appeared, a true Air Cavalry was born. Though most of the USAF machines are gone, the army expects to keep the Huey through the first decade of the new century.

1989
Lockheed C-5B Galaxy

The vast maw of the C-5 slowly swings open to reveal an interior resembling a 150-foot section of the Holland Tunnel. The Galaxy's slab-sided fuselage is mated to surprisingly petite wings and a high-flying tail, all rolling on 32 wheels—a super cargo mover. Though plagued by cost over-runs and weight problems when introduced in 1969, and with an under-strength wing that would later haunt its builders, the Galaxy has proved itself in Vietnam, Israel's Yom Kippur War, and, of course, the Persian Gulf, where they carried more than 230,000 tons of supplies during Desert Shield and Desert Storm.

When routine tests began showing fatigue cracks in the C-5's wings in the early eighties, Lockheed devised a program to "re-wing" every Galaxy in the inventory. The production lines were opened again in 1985 for a new batch of C-5Bs, using the new technology wings and a host of other improvements. In April 1989, the last of fifty

was handed over to Military Airlift Command at Dover Air Force Base, Delaware. The issue now is not whether the Galaxy can serve on into the second decade of the 21st century as planned, but whether the newly downsized air force crews can contend with their heavy transport workloads.

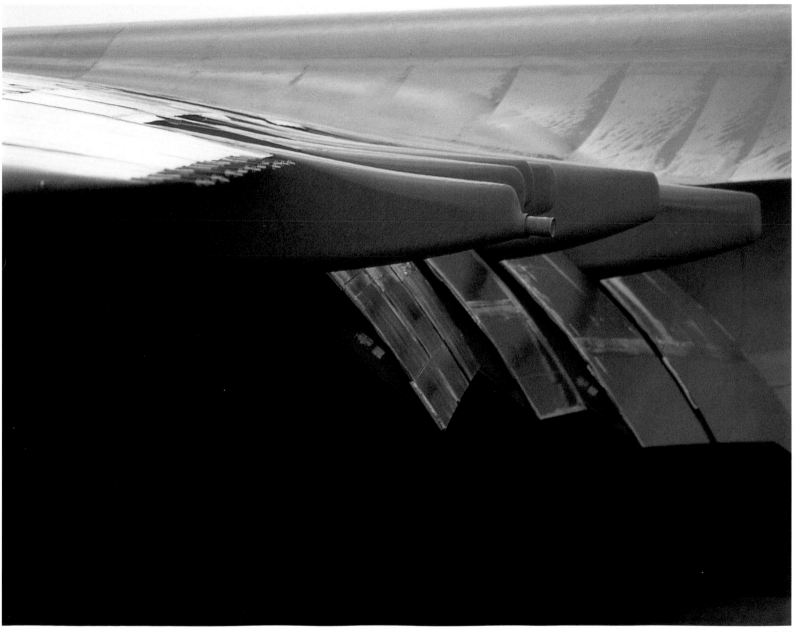

1990
Beech Super King Air

A Beech Super King Air of a small charter air line catches the last rays of sun at La Guardia Airport in New York City. The Super King Air, which first flew in 1972, is a direct descendant of the Queen Air of the fifties and the King Air of the sixties, small business twins which are themselves related, distantly, to the prewar Beechcraft 18 twin. Its most recognizable feature is its jet-like T-tail. Rivals from Cessna and Piper were seriously trounced and so far almost 2,000 have been produced with offspring such as the Model 1900 regional airliner also selling well.

Though the armed forces version of the Super King Air, called the C-12 Huron, is anything but warlike, the C-12 found itself embroiled in two military actions during 1990. In January, some C-12s could be spotted at Howard Air Force Base, Panama during "Operation Just Cause" and, as the year ended, a few Super King Airs joined the "Desert Shield" build up in Saudi Arabia. The army, air force, and navy together have acquired 450 of these versatile planes.

1990-2000

As the century ends some see
the airplane as commonplace.
But the excitement is still there,
from sleek executive transport
and stealthy Gulf war veteran,
to new dreams of exotic
anti-gravity craft.

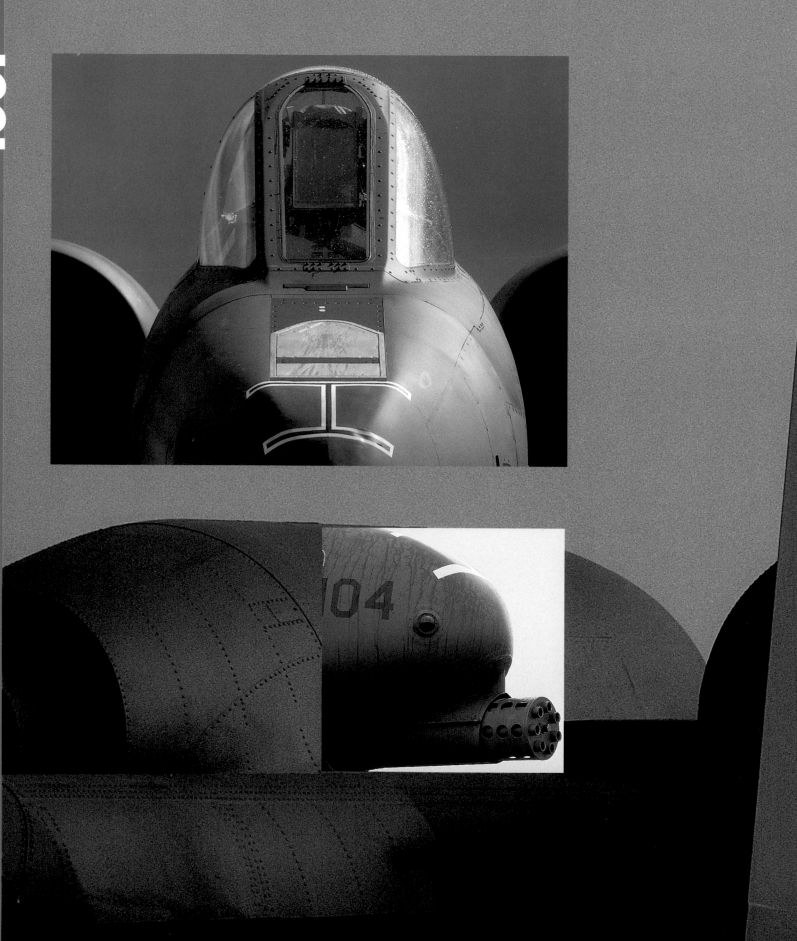

1991
Fairchild A-10
Warthog

Of all the craft that went to war in the Persian Gulf as the ground phase of "Desert Storm" got started in February 1991, none were more welcome over the heads of the U.S. troops than the Fairchild A-10.

The A-10 is an ugly beast, a "Warthog," which pilots maintain is "built out of old B-25 parts." Indeed, the design does have a decided World War II tang to it, when compared to the dart-like silhouettes of fighter planes such as the F-16. However, the Fairchild A-10 is no flying dinosaur; beneath the "lizard scheme" camouflage is a high-tech warplane built to survive the lethal shooting gallery that

exists over modern battlefields. The Warthog was literally designed around its gun, a twenty-foot-long, tank-killing cannon that spews massive Coke-bottle sized uranium bullets at over four thousand rounds a minute.

The A-10 is also designed to bring its pilot home. The pilot's cockpit is a "bathtub" of titanium armor, proof against 23mm. cannon fire. An entire engine can be shot from its mounting, one rudder or a third of a wing can be lost, and if a crash landing is necessary, the partly exposed wheels of the landing gear minimize danger.

153

1992
Lockheed F-117A Night Hawk

By 1992, in the middle of a giant U.S. Air Force organizational shake up, most Gulf War veteran F-117s had rotated back to Holloman Air Force Base in the States, leaving small detachments in Saudi Arabia to enforce the No-Fly Zone.

Another spooky product of Lockheed's Skunk Works, which some say employs extraterrestrial engineers, the F-117 resembles no other airplane ever built.— and it is quite likely nothing like it will ever be built again. Its faceted appearance, though designed to scatter radar signals, results from the inability of the computer programs used in its design to handle curved surfaces. As hundreds of Iraqi anti-aircraft gunners can attest, however, stealth works! Every system, almost every part, was designed with stealth in mind. Engine intakes are screened to prevent radar returns from the turbines, jet exhausts are widened and directed upward in a "platypus tail" to attenuate infrared hot spots, and radar absorbing material, or RAM, coats all surfaces.

Most of these measures are truly effective only at night, and that is when the F-117 strikes. On the morning of January 17, 1991, Night Hawks hit command and control objectives near Baghdad. Though first estimates of effectiveness were over-optimistic, up to 80 percent of their attacks took out their target.

1993
McDonnell Douglas F-15 Eagle

Air action was centered in Bosnia in 1993, and the U.S. Air Force's F-15 Eagle was in the thick of things. F-15Cs based in Aviano, Italy, were tasked with Operation Deny Flight missions until the end of July.

As air combat reports from Vietnam came in during the late sixties, it became evident that the air force's next fighter plane must have both missiles and guns. The picture here shows infra-red seeking Sidewinders under the wing of an early Eagle which, combined with the radar guided Sparrow missile, made a very effective one-two punch in the Gulf War. Thirty-five kills were scored by F-15s against the Iraqis with no air-to-air losses, proving that the Eagle is a superb dogfighter in spite of its hulking size. Size translates into weight-carrying ability as well, so the Eagle can "get down to earth" as a bomber.

1994 General Dynamics   F-16

1994-1995

Heir to Korea's Sabre Jet and World War II's Mustang for the title of "Cadillac of the Air," the sleek Falcon was the result of a competition in 1975 for a new lightweight fighter to complement the big F-15 Eagle. When the F-16 won the fly-off against the Northrop YF-17, her futuristic lines were obviously revolutionary. But the "Viper," as she is nicknamed by her crews, was also first with fly by wire controls, a one-piece frameless canopy, and a video-game-like side-stick controller. The Viper grew in size and complexity, but it became the standard NATO fighter for four nations later in 1975. Other countries jumped aboard, including Israel, which was the first to use Falcons in combat, in a 1981 attack on Iraq.

The Gulf War of 1991 was not a high point for the Falcon, as it was more and more burdened with tons of "mud-moving" iron slung under its wings in ground attack missions. "The Boys from Syracuse," the 138th Fighter Squadron of the New York Air National Guard shown in the large photo, were in the thick of it on bombing runs. Though they suffered no losses, five other F-16s were shot down in the battle.

1995
Rockwell B-1B Lancer

The story goes that the B-1B got its nickname of "The Bone" when a journalist left the hyphen out of "B-one" in a story, and aircrews leapt upon the name with glee. The name seems to fit: from many vantage points, the long, area-ruled fuselage and the organic curves of its wing fillets resemble some fossilized monster thighbone. And the controversial plane, always a "bone of contention," is now the "backbone" of the bomber fleet.

Begun in the sixties as a B-52 replacement, the original B-1A flew in 1974, but was cancelled in 1977 by President Jimmy Carter before production could start. In 1981, President Ronald Reagan revived the bomber as the B-1B. It was now to be a sub-sonic, low-level penetrator, with some stealth features, and it would carry nuclear cruise missiles. The "Bone" has been dogged by problems with poor terrain following, radar jamming, and structural failures, among others, all tracked hungrily by the media. To counter bad press, the air force has used the B-1 to break numerous records, most notable being a 36-hour, non-stop, around-the-world flight in June 1995.

The mysterious explosion and crash of TWA Flight 800 on July 17, 1996, raised grim questions about the safety of some of the older Boeing 747s. The monster plane had been one of the industry's safest since its introduction in 1970.

In all, more than 1,200 have been delivered, and the 747's share of the Jumbo market is basically 100 percent, since its only real competitor—the Airbus 340—is quite a bit smaller. Rumblings from Airbus of its huge, double-decked A-3XX, with room for 600 passengers, were answered with denials from Boeing that any new plane would replace the 747. By the end of 1996, it looked as though Boeing had settled upon offering a stretch of the basic 747 airframe in its models 747-500 and 747-600, using a brand-new wing and grossing over one million pounds, but requiring no major changes in airport handling.

Meanwhile 747s such as this early Pan Am model and a later version at Seattle's SETAC airport continue to labor worldwide as the world's foremost people movers.

1997
Cessna 120/170 Series

After a hiatus of more than a decade, the return of the all-time, best-selling light plane, the Cessna 172, to production in 1997 highlighted the resurgence of the private flying community as the nineties drew to a close. The new product liability laws limiting punitive legal judgments which had been driving general aviation's remaining companies toward bankruptcy didn't hurt either. This is a great comeback for Cessna, which had been building single-engine cabin monoplanes since the late twenties.

Illustrated here is the true ancestor of the 172, the metal-framed, two-seat 120/140 series, first flown in 1945, whose combination of low price and relatively high power led it to top spot in the post war sales boom and eventually created the ever-expanding Cessna dynasty of today—small business twins, single-engine utility transports, agricultural planes, air force and navy trainers, and assorted corporate business jets. The 1955 series 170 was a four-seat version of the petite 120, which begat the tricycle-geared 172, and so on up to the dandified Skyhawk and 182 models with all manner of variations. The little Cessna has become Everyman's lightplane. All told, counting military trainer versions, upwards of 60,000 have flown.

1998
Boeing 777

Boeing has launched its envoy into the third millennium – the new 777 wide body twin jet, a plane that will no doubt be serving well into the middle of the twenty-first Century. Perceiving a gap in market position between its huge 747 jumbos and the mid-sized 767, and hoping to forestall competition, Boeing inaugurated this ocean spanning, 400 plus passenger heavyweight with unprecedented airline cooperation in 1990.

Though the 777 bears a strong resemblance to its earlier sibling the 767, the plane is totally new from its six-wheeled landing gear to its 747-400 inspired LCD "glass cockpit" and fly-by-wire digital controls. The 200 foot wing is also new, using a super efficient airfoil that, along with 90,000 pound thrust engines that sip less fuel, are keys to the 777's long range.

Boeing used its new computer-aided "paperless" three-dimensional design system for the 777, realizing savings in time and reduced prototyping delays, while easing introduction of the new team-oriented design approach. The debut flight was in 1995. These pictures show early prototypes in Boeing livery. By 1998 By 1998 the 777-300 was flying, a "stretched" version of the basic plane with a fuselage longer than the longest 747 now flying.

162

1999
Unpiloted Aircraft Concepts

Remotely guided or robot flying craft have been around since the latter days of World War I. Expendable surveillance drones are increasingly important over today's battlefield, though they are really just glorified radio controlled model airplanes. Rapid advances in micro-miniaturization of propulsion, guidance, and imaging, along with new composite materials and fabrication methods are opening new pathways to flight in the realm of both the very small and the very large.

One novel approach to micro air vehicle (MAV) propulsion is that of Dr. Robert Michelson and his associates at the Georgia Tech Research Institute. They reasoned that at scales of six inches and smaller, propellers and airfoils lose much of their efficiency, meaning that flapping insect like wings might perform best. Michelson's machine, called an entomopter, uses chemically powered "muscles" that expand and contract rapidly to flap its wings. Shown in the photo is a working model of these wings, while the diagram shows the proposed four inch long Mayfly-like machine that should fly later in 1998.

At the other end of the scale are huge but feather light solar powered craft built using Dr. Paul MacCready's pioneering methods for human powered flight. His company, AeroVironment, is working with NASA to build a 220 foot-span solar powered flying wing called the Centurion that, in later versions, will fly for days at a time at 100,000 feet. The Pathfinder, an earlier 100 foot span plane that reached over 70,000 feet.and a quarter scale battery powered model of the Centurion are illustrated. Using rechargeable storage cells to power the engines at night, planes like these could track storms and collect upper atmosphere data or serve as low cost communication relay stations.

2000
Gravity Modification
Experiments

The following article appeared in Aviation Week and Space Technology on 14 July 1997. We await further developments.

GRAVITY MODIFICATION EXPERIMENTS

A team working on NASA's Advanced Space Transportation Program is pursuing several small, "breakthrough physics" research projects that could have a significant effect on future space flight. The project's approach is to search out and review promising areas where experimental data from astronomy, astrophysics, particle physics and other fields does not fit accepted theories, according to Garry Lyles, manager of the ASTP program at Marshall Space Flight Center in Huntsville, Ala. Cleveland-based NASA-Lewis, however, is leading the breakthrough physics effort. Areas of interest include faster-than-light travel, inertia modification and quantum fluctuation energy. To qualify, ideas must have a well-developed theoretical basis, pass a peer review and have defined experiments that can provide low-cost, clear resolution to the theory. A first experiment, on potential gravity modification, is being pursued in conjunction with the University of Alabama and should be completed by year-end. If successful, it could help shield an object from its gravitational field, effectively lowering the weight of launcher or orbital vehicles and reducing the need for heavy-lift boosters. NASA plans a closed, mid-August workshop to recommend which subjects to pursue.

What of The Next Century of Flight?

Will the growing longevity of current aircraft and the prohibitive costs of developing new ones mean that the aircraft of the next century will be a dull re-hash of today's planes ad infinitum? Don't count on it! Right now, behind the scenes, an amazing surge in creativity is shaping aeronautical development in almost every field. Led by the once torpid private flying sector and the Experimental Aircraft Association, a powerful grass-roots organization that encourages innovation among amateur plane builders and small plane owners, every aspect of private flying is advancing: new engines, from converted auto engines to tiny but powerful jets; new uses for composite materials and plastics such as pioneered by Burt Rutan; new affordable precision electronics using global satellite positioning for navigation and collision avoidance.

Even in the world of civil transport, where after decades of dull aluminum tubes and diminishing competition, research is beginning into more capacious, more fuel efficient airliners. Also, new supersonic transport designs, more environmentally friendly and less noisy than the aging Concorde are on drawing boards (or computer screens) at Boeing and in Europe. A civil version of the tilt-wing military XV-22 transport has been ordered in quantity before it has even flown. Non-polluting fuels such as hydrogen are close to flight testing. In the immediate future, we have seen how Boeing and its rival Airbus are planning 600 seat versions of their existing planes.

On the horizon might be a revival of the aerospace plane or "Orient Express" that was championed by President Ronald Reagan. A one-stage-to-orbit, or cross-Pacific ram-jet-powered passenger plane might just be possible in the first half of the century. Certain dreams, however, such as the return of the dirigible, which seems always to be imminent to some dreamers, and the arrival of huge flying wings or "span-loaders," have been put aside for the foreseeable future.

The military, hamstrung by budget cuts, has responded by re-thinking their need for piloted aircraft. Though certain advanced conventional planes such as the Lockheed Martin F-22, which has just flown in production form, are on deck as replacements for some of the aging planes U.S. forces are flying, other equally elderly planes, such as the B-52 bomber and the T-38 trainer have no replacement in sight. Unpiloted or "uninhabited" planes, as the Defense Department like to call them, may be the solution. Another way for the military to

get more bang for the buck is to accelerate the trend toward smarter weapons, both with improved laser guided bombs like those used in Desert Storm, and new wide-area cluster munitions — "Sensor Fused Weapons"— that enable a single warplane to cover a twenty football field area and deliver 1,200 weapons in one pass. Of course for those craft that still require pilots, the cockpit environment is quickly evolving into a helmet mounted "total immersion" virtual display.

Stealth, as championed by the U.S. Air Force seems to have been dismissed as irrelevant by the navy and by European forces, but this might be merely a case of sour grapes. The Russians are rumored to have something stealthy in the works, however.

The tiny micro-air-vehicles discussed earlier in the book seem to have extremely unsettling implications for our privacy, and if NASA's experiments in anti-gravity bear fruit, then all bets are off and all our predictions become invalid. The only thing sure is that the next hundred years will definitely not be a replay of the first century of flight!

List of Airplane and Aerospace Museums and Aircraft Collections

These museums are the ones actually visited in the course of shooting the photos for this book. We thank the many dedicated individuals at these fantastic institutions who over the years have assisted us. Of course there are many other fine collections throughout the world that are also worth a visit.

Battleship Alabama Memorial Park
PO Box 65
Mobile AL 36601
205-433-2703

•Breckenridge Aviation Museum
(Confederate Air Force collection)
PO Box 308
Breckenridge TX 76024
817-559-3201

Cradle of Aviation Museum
Museums at Mitchel Center
Museum Lane / Mitchel Field
Garden City NY 11530
516-572-0411

Intrepid Sea Air and Space Museum
Intrepid Square
New York NY 10036
212 245 0072

March Field Museum
22 AREFW/CVM
March AFB, Riverside CA 92518-5000
714-655-3725

•Mid Atlantic Air Museum
RD 9 Box 9381
Reading PA 19605
215-372-7333

Museum of Flight
9404 East Marginal Way South
Seattle WA 98108
206-764-5720

National Air and Space Museum
6th Street & Independence Ave SW
Washington DC 20560
202-357-2700

New England Air Museum
Bradley International Airport
Windsor Locks CT 06096
203-623-3305

•Old Rhinebeck Aerodrome
42 Stone Church Road
Rhinebeck NY 12572
914-758-8610

•Owls Head Transportation Museum
PO Box 277
Owl's Head ME 04854
207-594-4418

Pima Air and Space Museum
6000 E Valencia RD
Tucson AZ 85706
602-574-9658

San Diego Aerospace Museum
2001 Pan American Plaza, Balboa Park
San Diego CA 92101
619-234-8291

•Weeks Fantasy of Flight Musem
Polk City FL ...
813-984-3500

•Canadian Warbird Heritage Museum
PO Box 35, Mount Hope
Ontario Canada LOR 1WO
416-679-4183

•Duxford Airfield
Duxford Cambridge CB2 4QR
UK
01223 835000

•The Shuttleworth Collection
Old Warden Aerodrome
Bigglesworth Befordshire SG18 9ER
UK
01767 627288

French Aerospace Museum
Le Musée de l'Air et de l'Espace
Aéroport du Bouget
BP 73
93350 Le Bourget
FRANCE
1 838.91.11

Those collections that keep their aircraft in flying condition are bulleted.

Photo Credits

Pages 84-87   photos by Ed Vebell

Pages 123,123,144
                 Jon Lopez photos

Pages 160,161
                 photos courtesy of the
                 Boeing Company

Page 162,163   Entomopter photos
                 courtesy Robert
                 Michelson and Stanley
                 Leary of Georgia Tech.
                 Aerovironment
                 Pathfinder and Centurion
                 photos from NASA

Page 163   Reprinted from Aviation
                 Week and Aerospace
                 Technology, used with
                 permission

Acknowledgments and Thanks

To Mrs. Cole Palen and all the helpful folks up in Rhinebeck, including Jim Hare and the Cassens (both father and son),Dr. Anderson and his P-40, Gee Bee owner Delmar Benjamin, Kermit Weeks and staff, Ben Owen at EAA , Josh Stoff and Rebecca Looney at the Cradle of Aviation, Dr. Rob Michelson at Georgia Tech., Martin Crowley at Aerovironment, Jerry Roberts, Frank DeSisto, and Sev Mendez at the Intrepid, Bill Hooper at the New England Air Museum, David Van der Wal, Gordon McKinzie, Morton Hunt, and Ida Hawkins at Boeing, Alan and Fred Brown at NASA, Mary Francis Koerner at Aviation Week, Lou at Ace, David and Flora Persky, Deborah Leeds and Kate Aldinger at Imergy, Andy Kotsch, Marisa Bulzone, Ed Vebell, Jon Lopez.